No. Superhero

Ole Marius Joergensen

COLLECTIVE SHORTS
by NHP PUBLISHING

This book is to my uncle, Olav Folke Hauge.
Thanks for being the salesman and much more.

— Ole Marius Joergensen

Ole Marius Joergensen grew up in suburban Norway, where he and his friends roamed free in the neighborhood gardens and nearby mountains. He describes his childhood as "easy and uncomplicated" but marked an unquenchable thirst for unknown. He loved American popular culture but, much to his frustration, the extraordinary adventures he saw in Steven Spielberg's movies, always remained just out of his reach.

As an adult, Joergensen has returned to the area where he spent his youth, and he's also revisited the themes that captured his imagination in those early days. Throughout the years, Joergensen has created his own set of mysterious characters: the spaceman, the superhero, the traveling salesmen, and the sleepy figures that appear here and there throughout *A long forgotten Nocturne*.

However, in Joergensen's world, unlike Spielberg's, the heroes are defined, at least in part, by their ordinariness. The superhero can't fly, but he keeps trying, much like the artist himself has as a boy. And failing to launch into the cosmos, the astronaut is content with exploring the landscapes near his own home. When asked what ties all of his characters together, the artist responds, "They have a Nordic simplicity to them."

The solitary people who inhabit his lush and rural dreamscapes are both familiar and anonymous, as if we've walked past them a thousand times and never asked their names. They have dreams and aspirations that haven't yet been realized and perhaps never will. At the same time, they are all lost somehow; a few are from another era, while others are just out of place. Alone, silent, and wandering, they could be ghosts.

Joergensen's photography reminds me of the imaginary friends I had as a child. For so long they were my secret companions, until one day, they were gone. As grown-ups, we know that life is no longer "easy and uncomplicated", and it rarely ever lives up to the adventure movies we saw as kids. But in these pages, perhaps we can find traces of what we've lost, whether it be magic, excitement, hope, ambition, or just the warm glow from a light left on, calling us home on a dark night.

— Ellyn Kail (Feature Shoot)

NO.
SUPERHERO

2014

A playful series with dark undertones, "No Superhero" is an ode to one of Ole Marius' childhood heroes.

"At the age of seven, I became obsessed with superheroes. I loved their meaningful and adventurous lives, and was captivated by their colorful costumes. ...I decided to make Superman the subject of a photo series. My project shows the character of Superman as a real human being, going after the impossible mission. His big dream is to fly, regardless of the results — it's trial and error."

Ole Marius views Superman as a metaphor for taking risk and the worry of failure. Each scene is depicted through a lens that captures childhood nostalgia with the hero as an ordinary man; a man who is struggling with the difficulties of flying as the viewer deals with the everyday struggle of chasing his own goals.

Like a child, the superhero is willing to go to any lengths to achieve his goals, in this case flying regardless of the consequences.

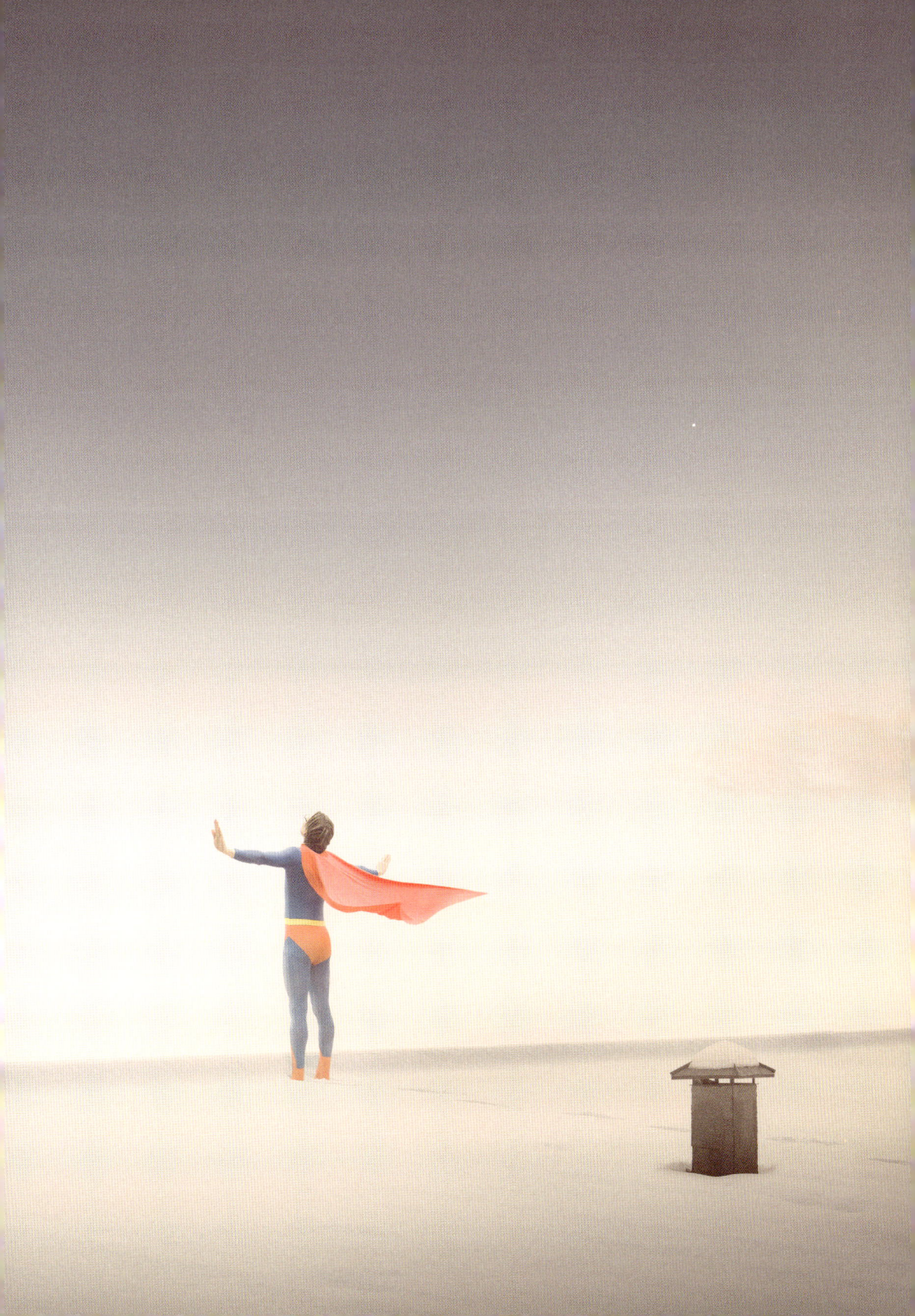

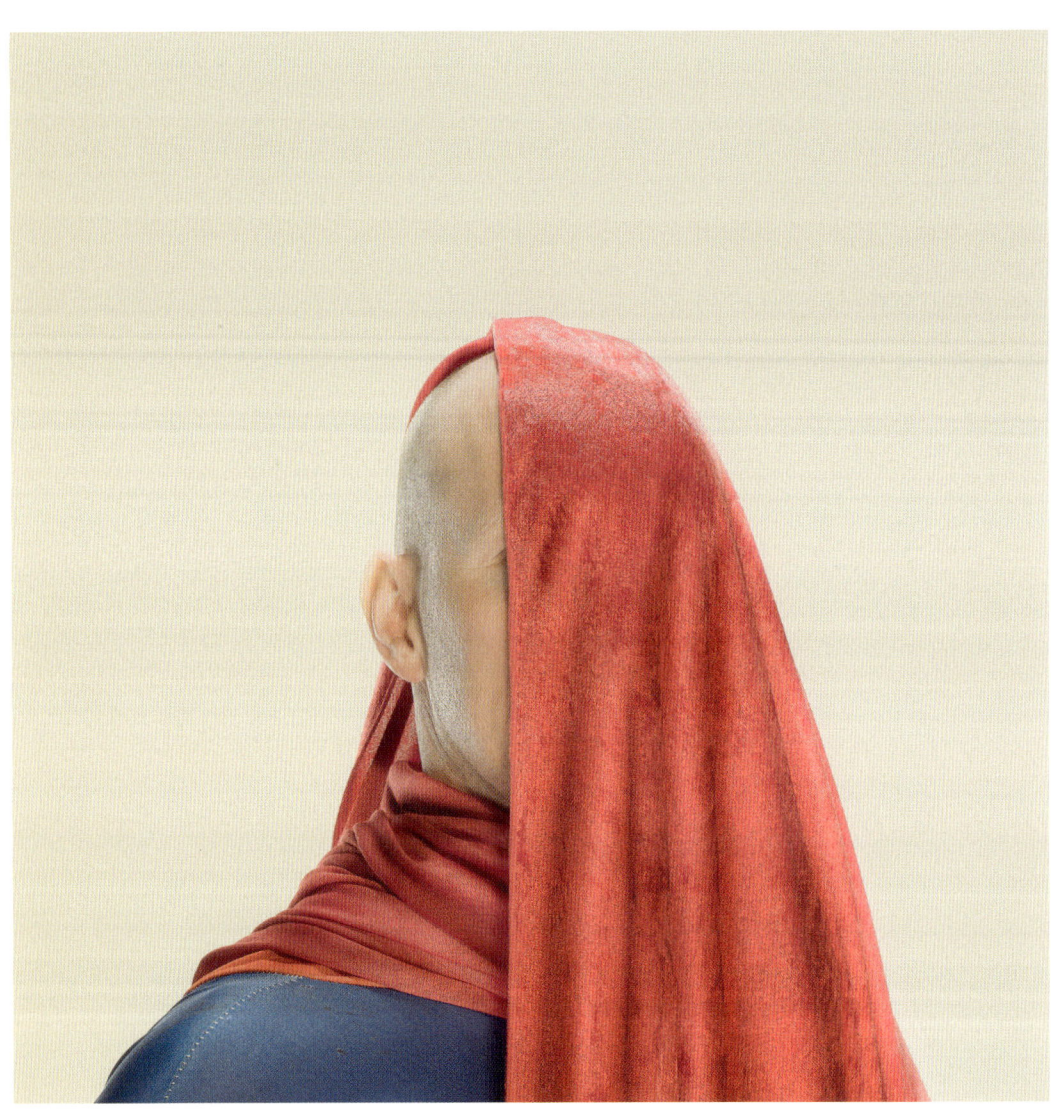

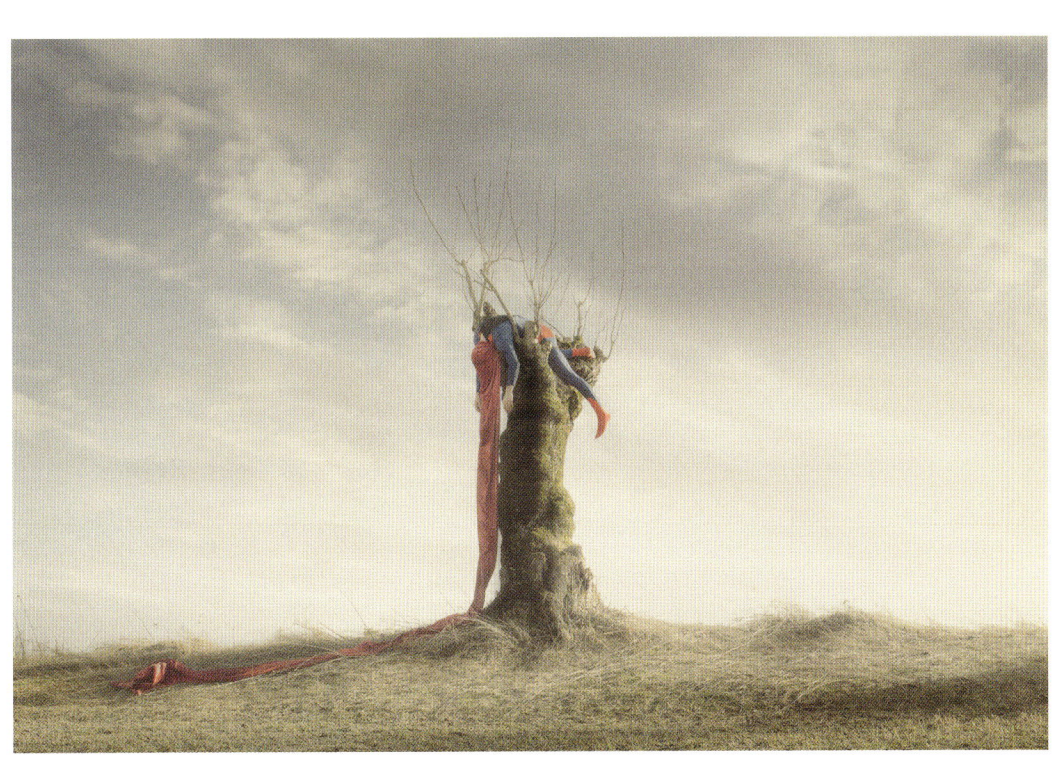

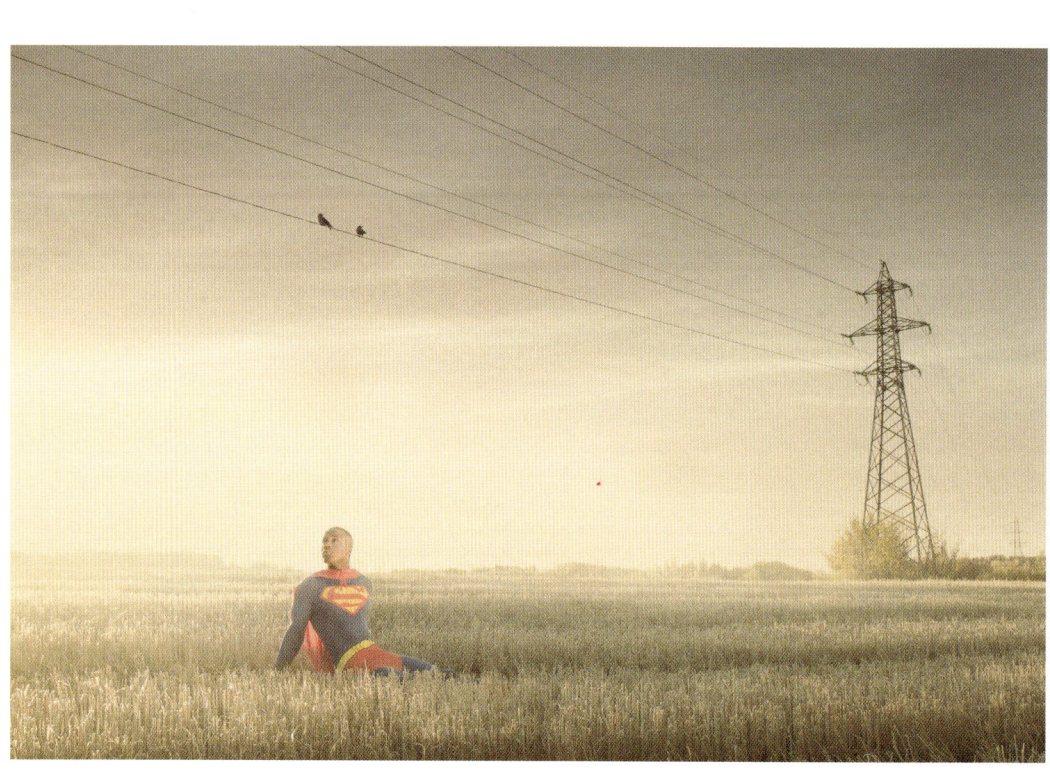

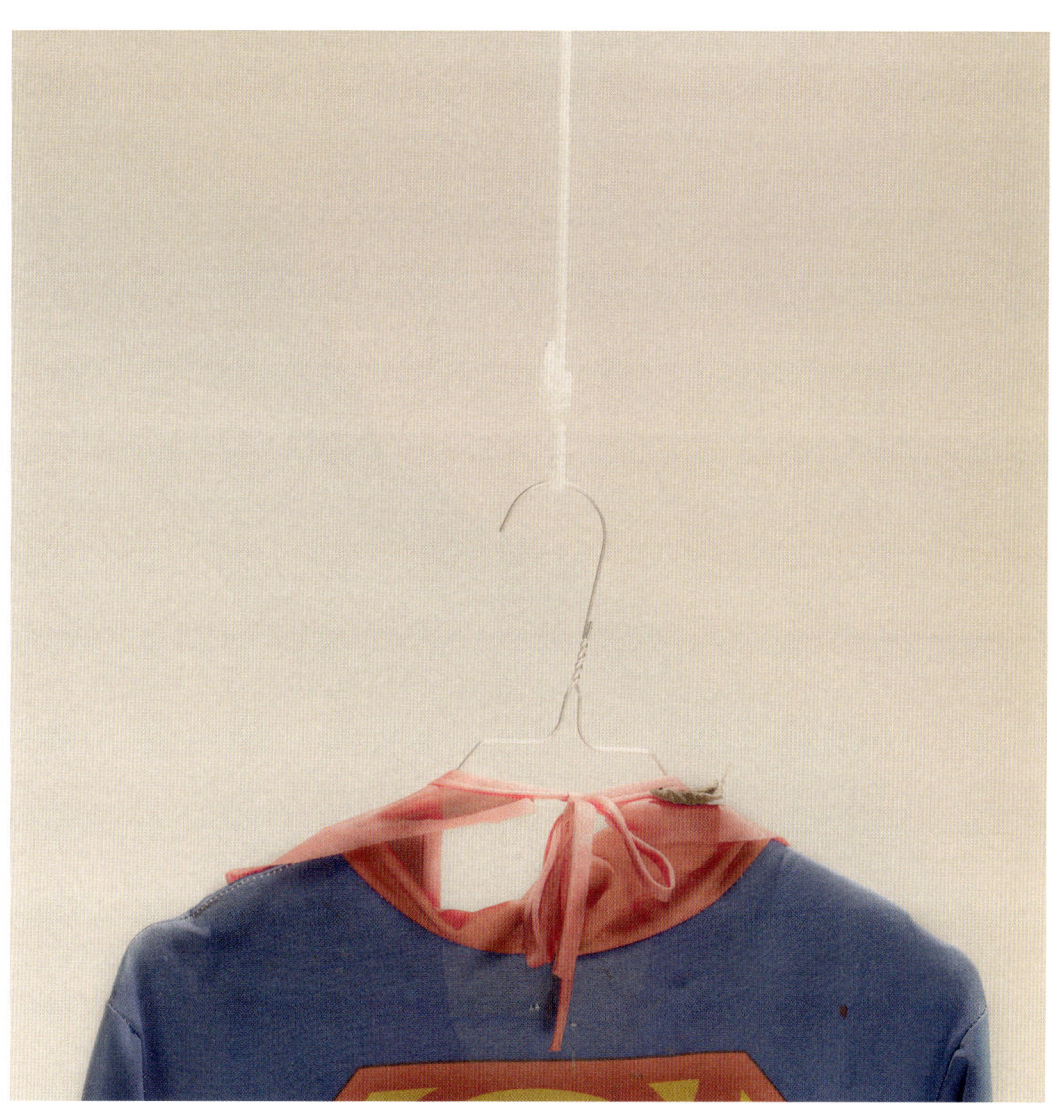

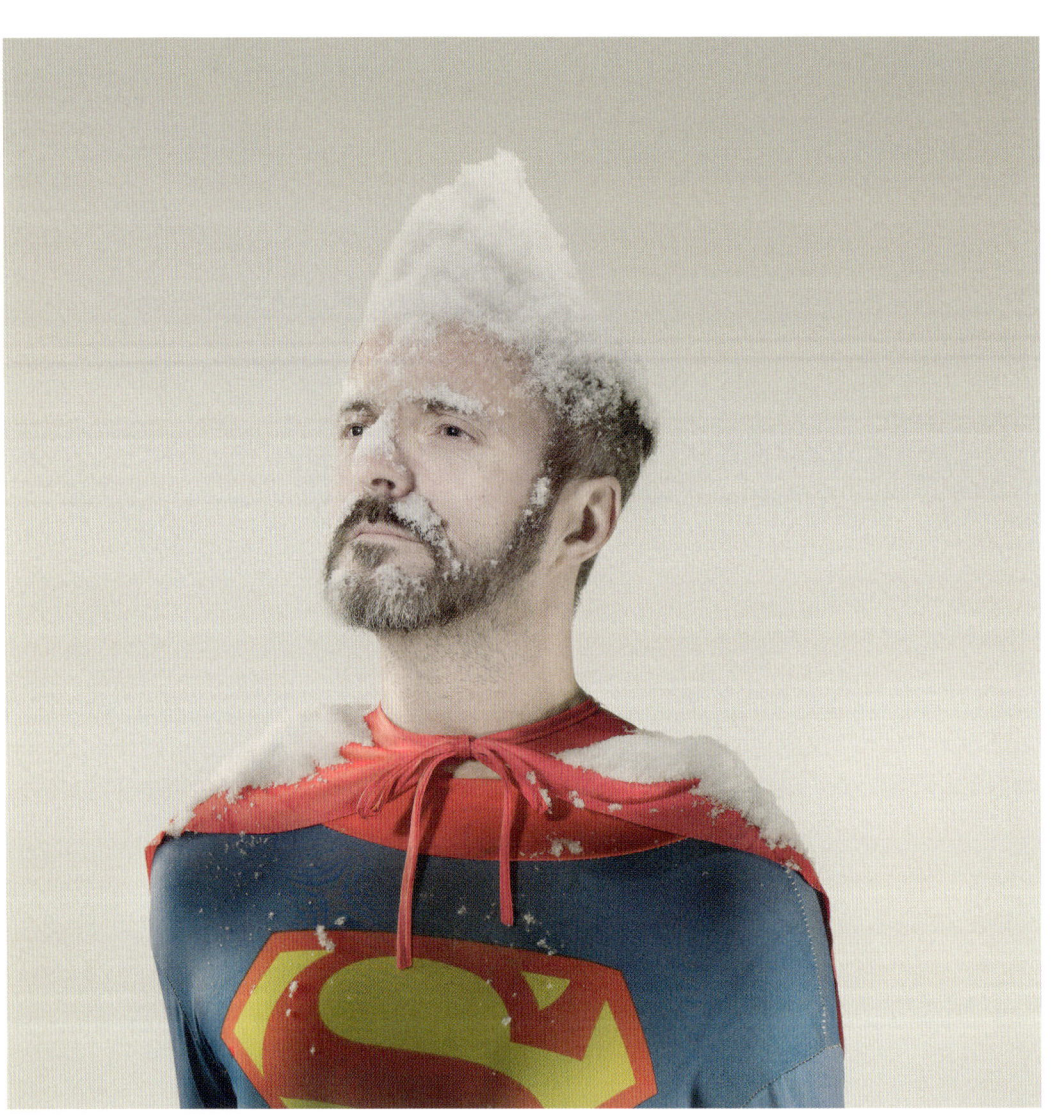

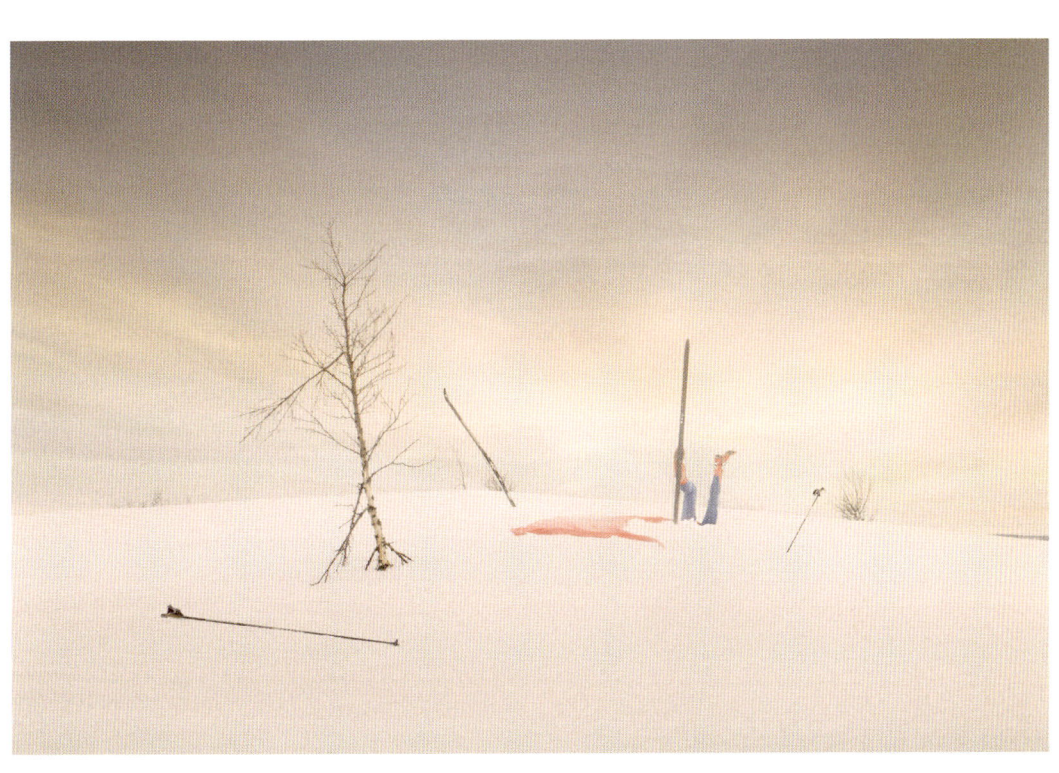

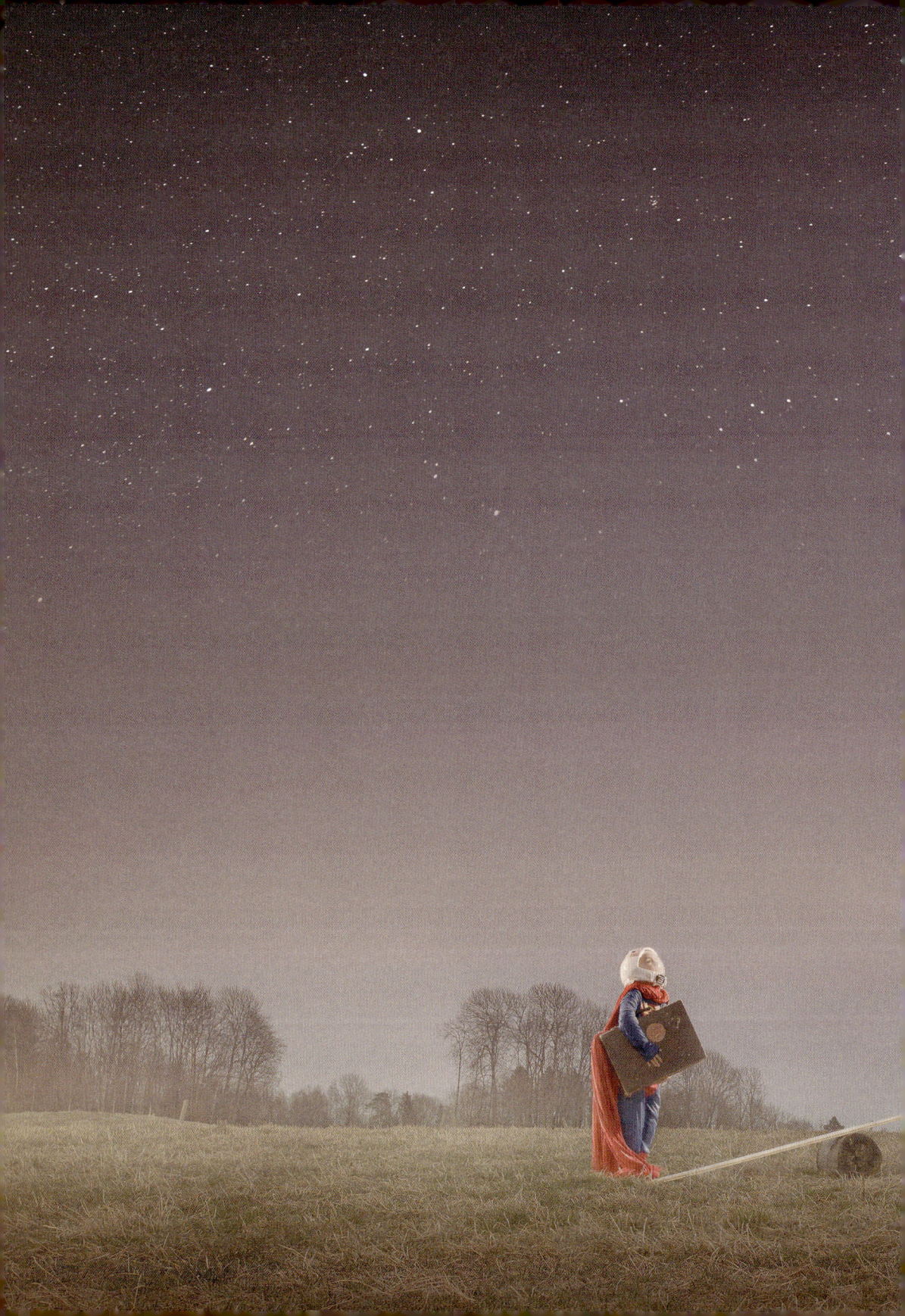

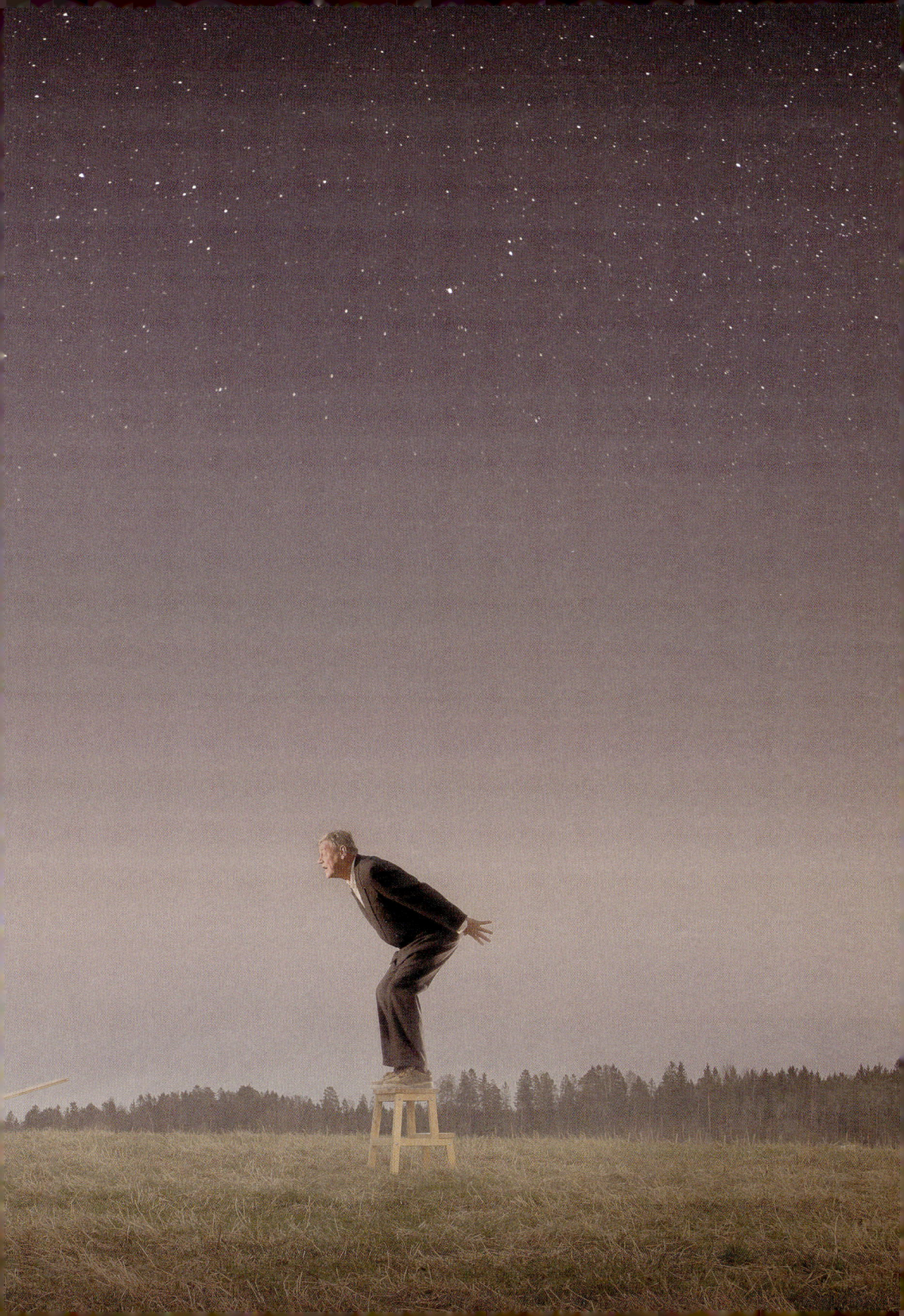

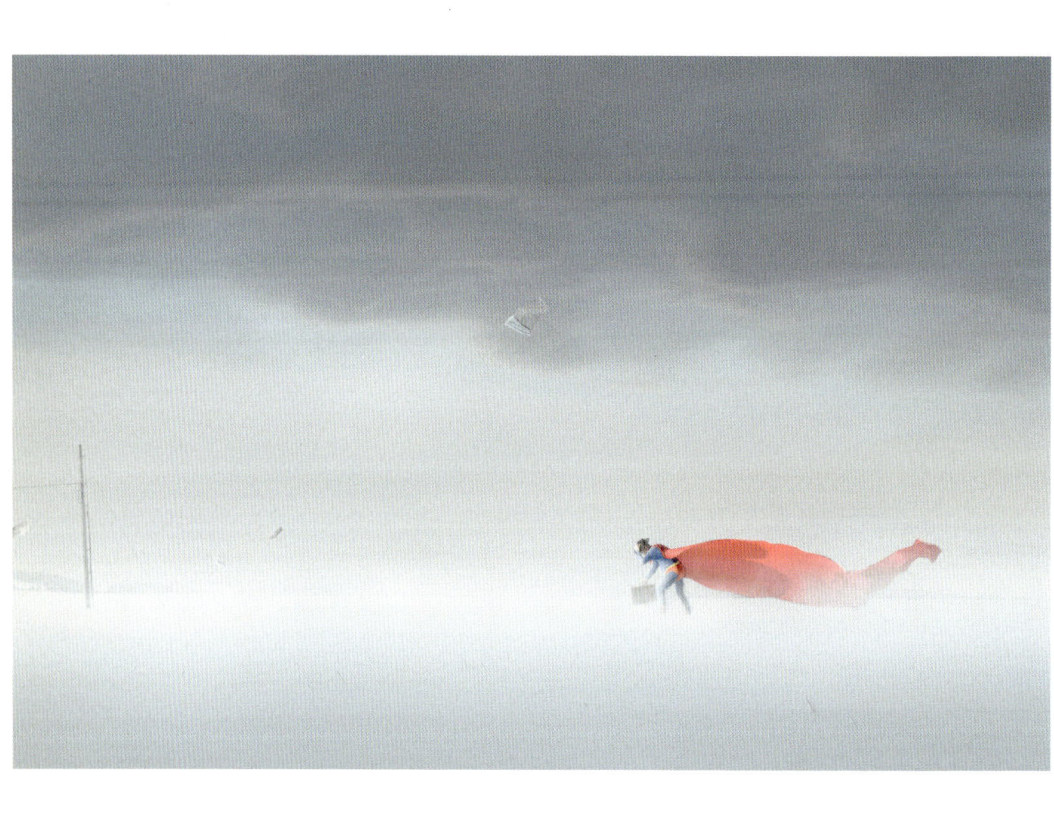

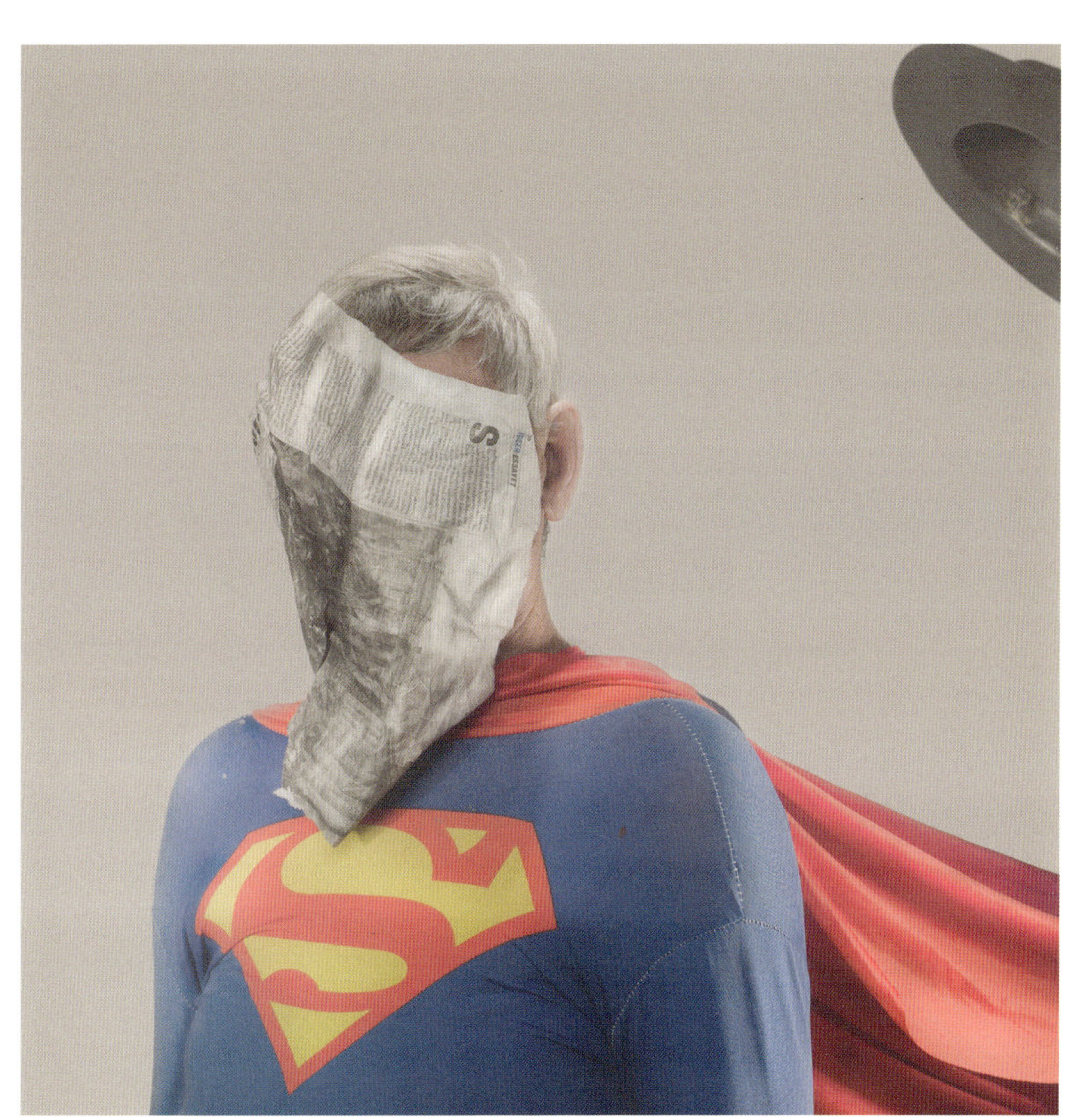

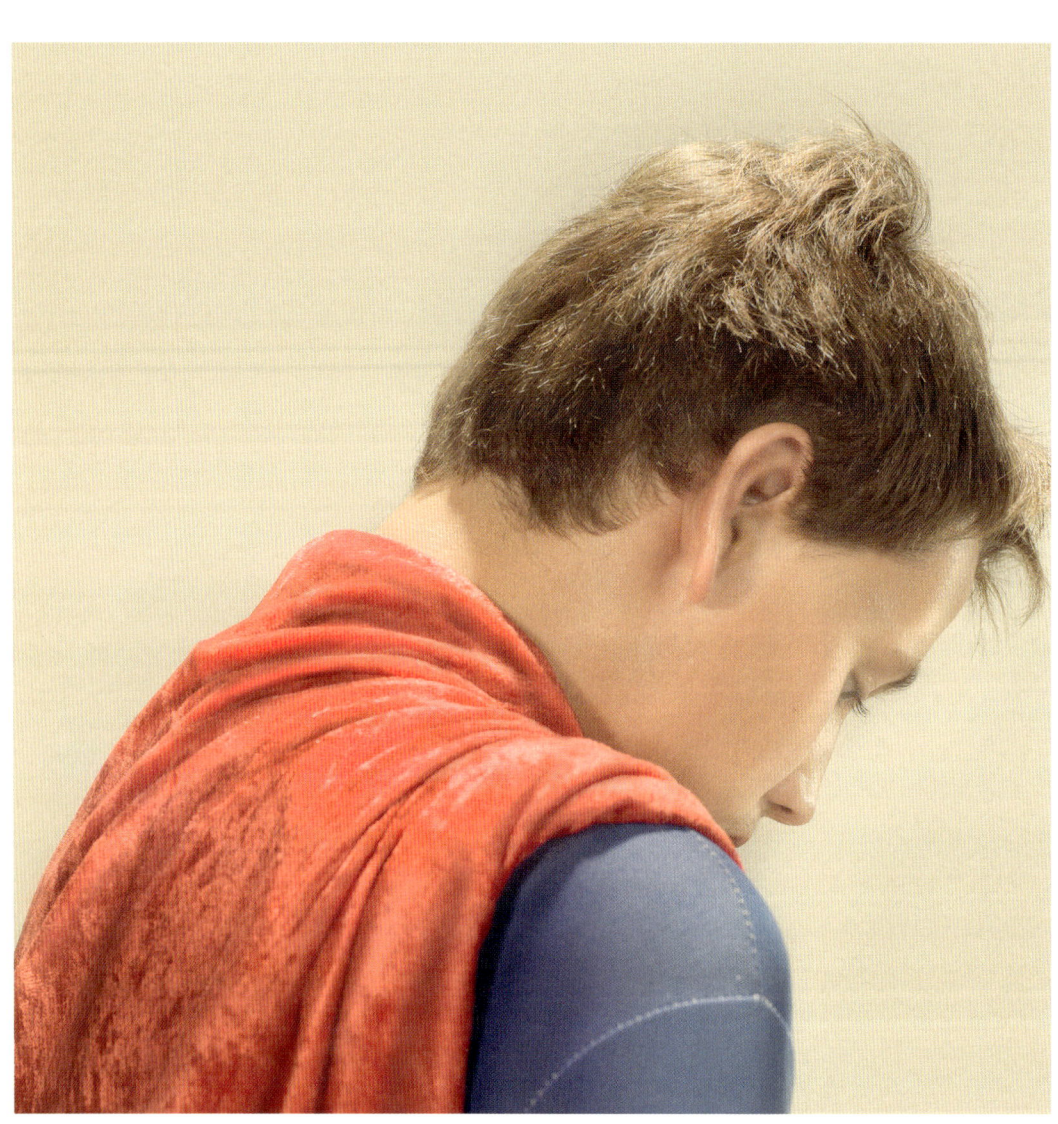

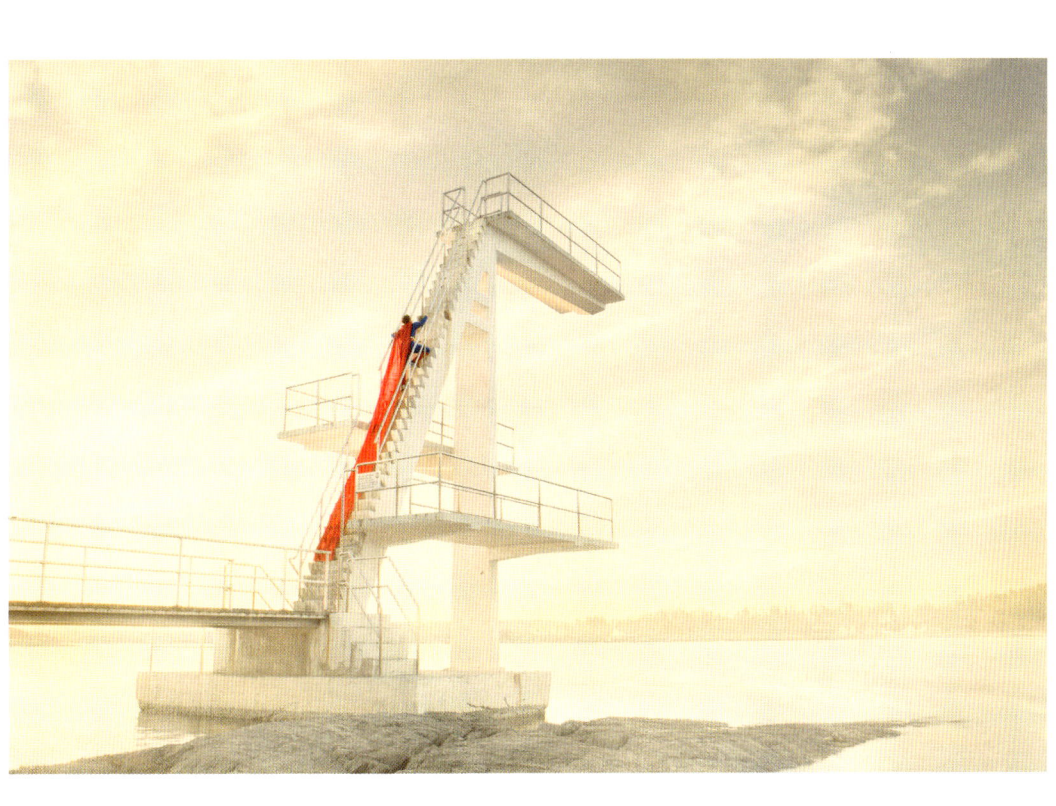

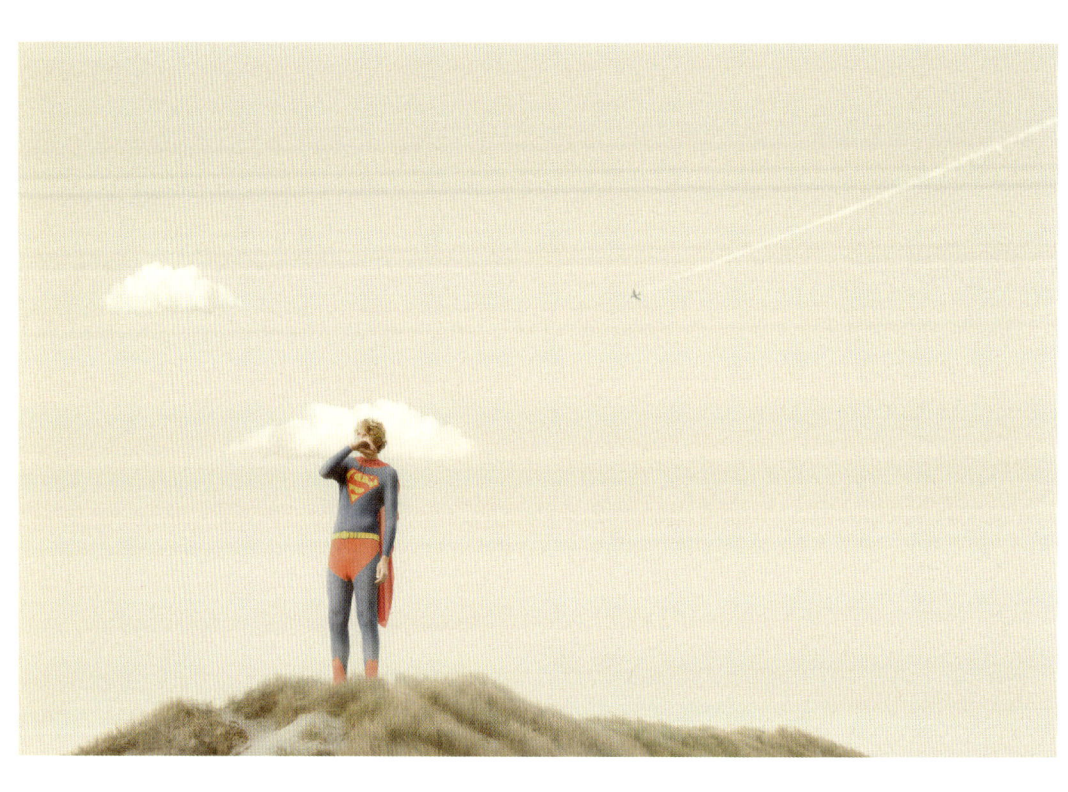

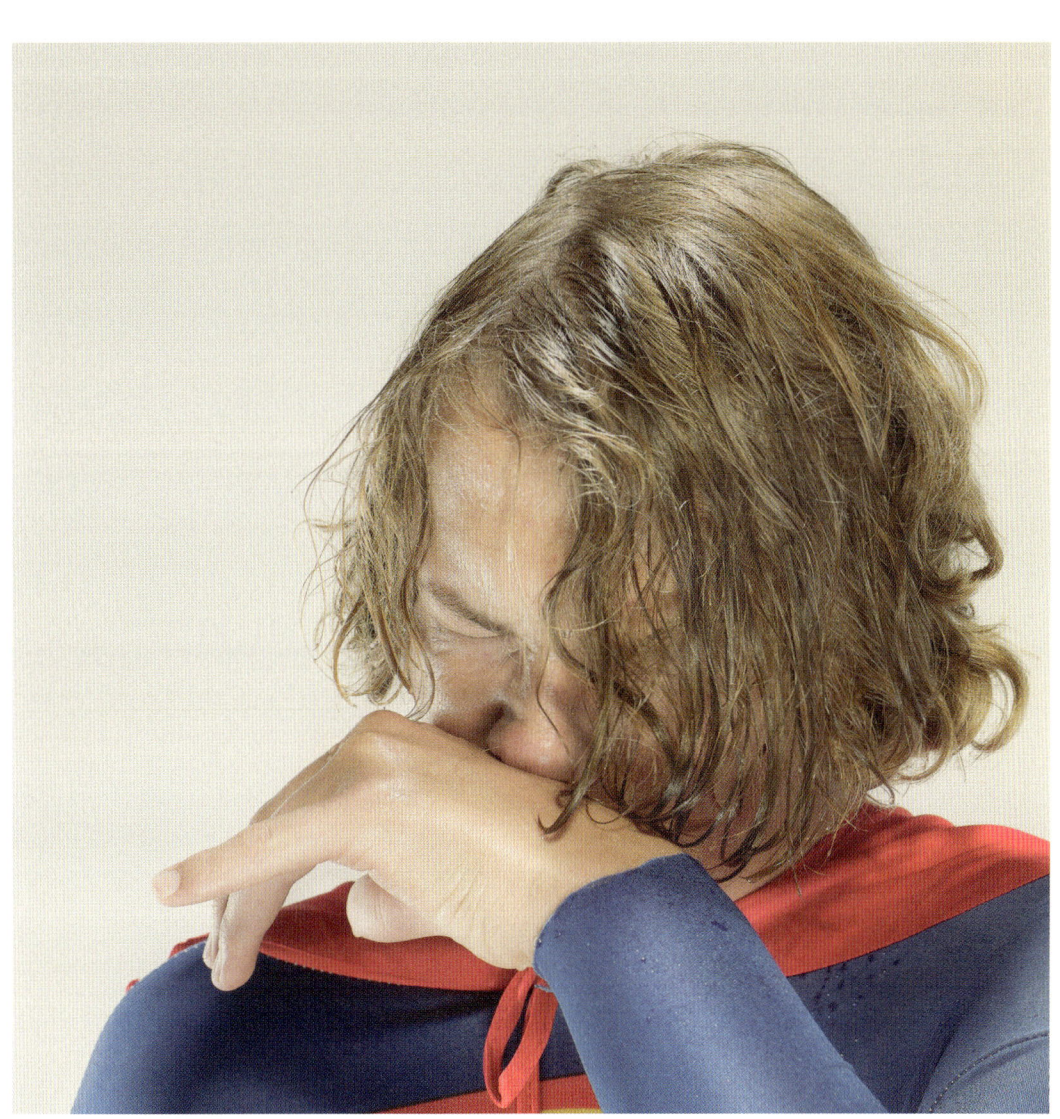

SPACE TRAVELS

2015–2017

In 2015, Ole Marius exhibited his "Space Travels" series, which was his unique rediscovery of his native country. The narrative is driven by the artist's desire to discover his homeland, and the protagonist's sense of confinement and helplessness tinged with humor.

"The idea was to play tourist, not only from a personal perspective but also as a humorous nod to the ways in which travelers like to pose in front of landscapes and landmarks."

For the artist, the spacesuit was a symbol for venturing into the unknown and charting new creative territories. It was a narrative driven by the sentiment of being trapped in a place and yearning for a new adventure that is out of reach.

Shot over a period of 2 years, exclusively in rural parts of Norway, with the help of a friend as a lonely astronaut, the series was a departure from his meticulously planned shoots. In this case, he found himself guided by the road and the new discovery around each corner.

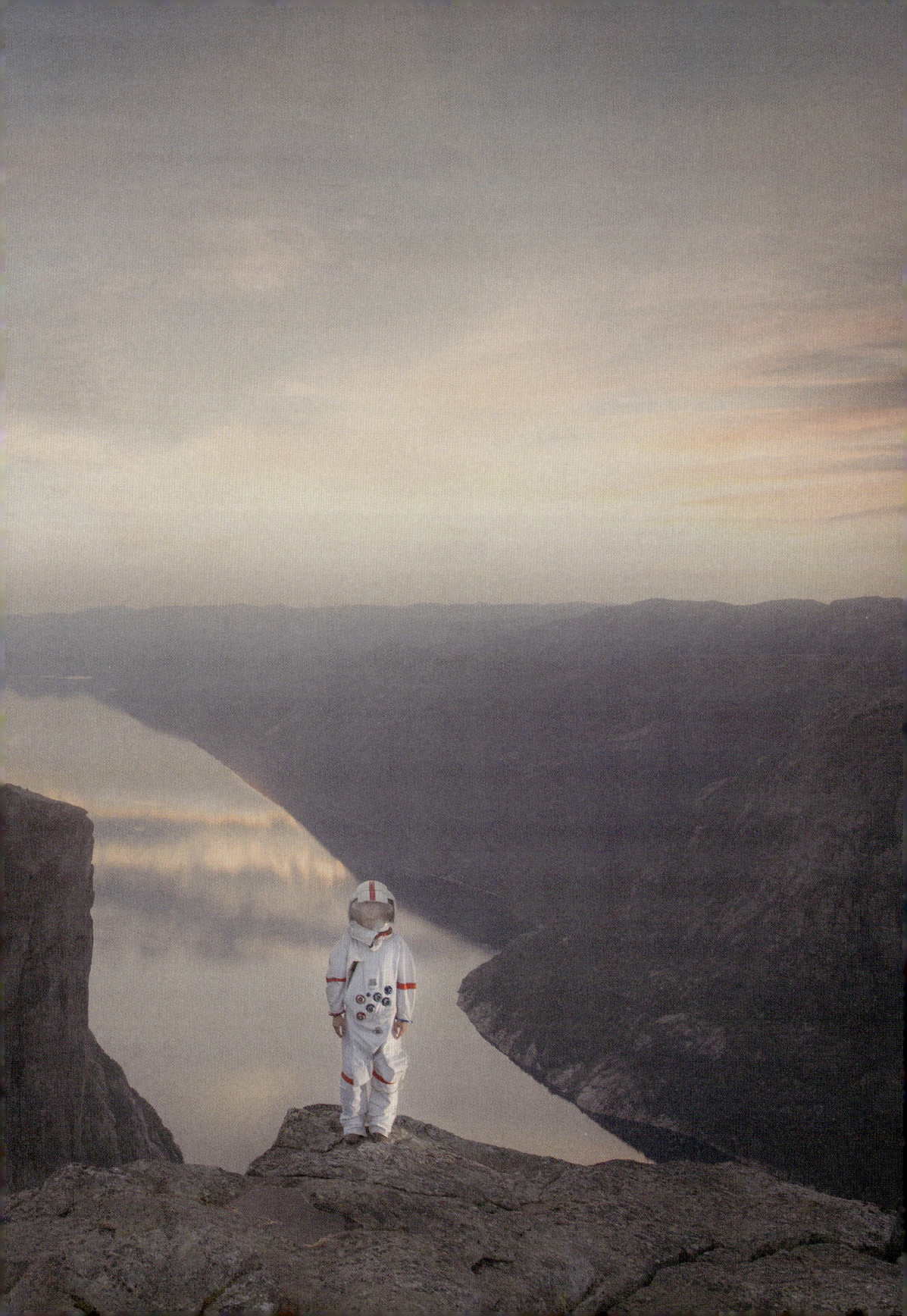

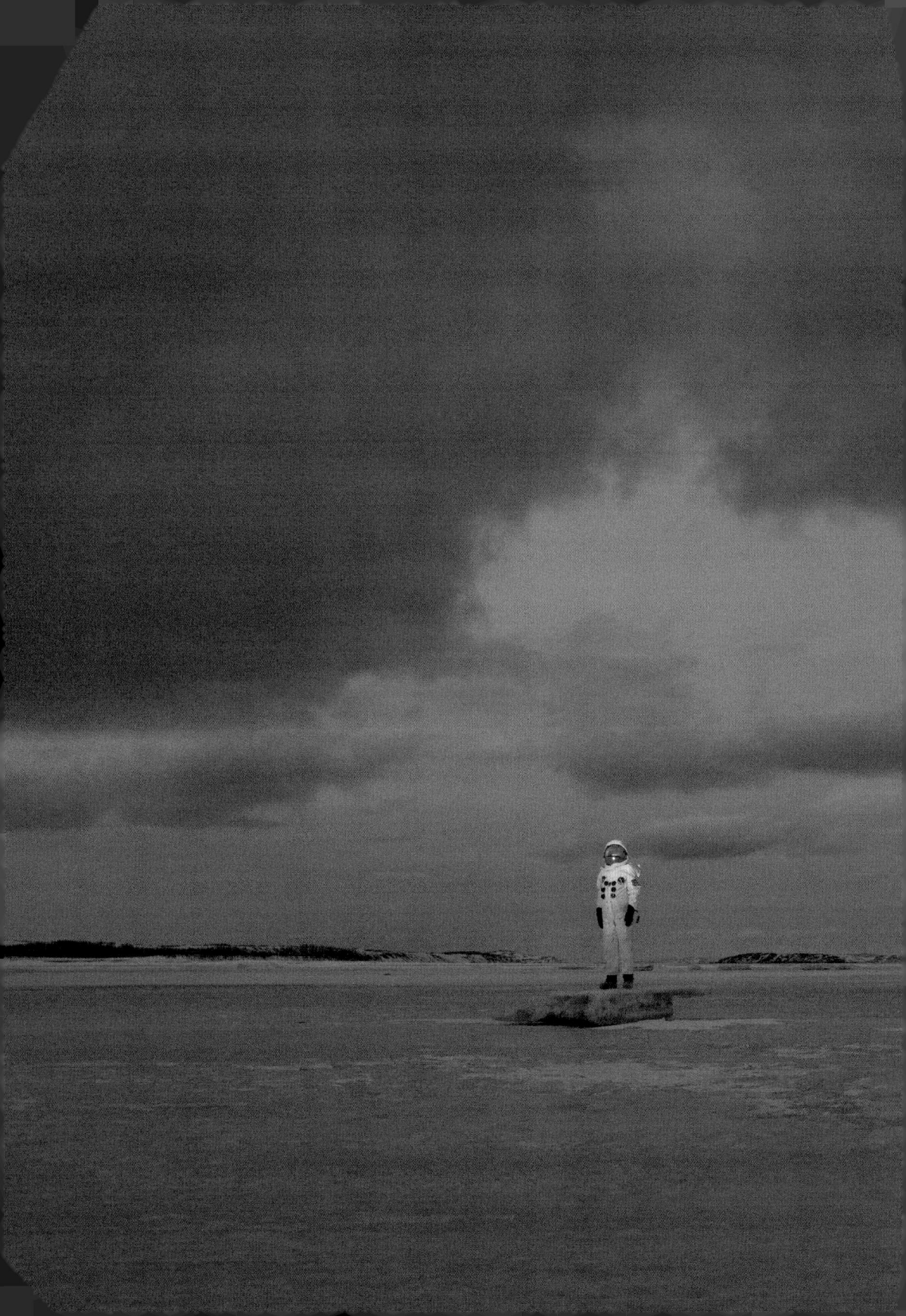

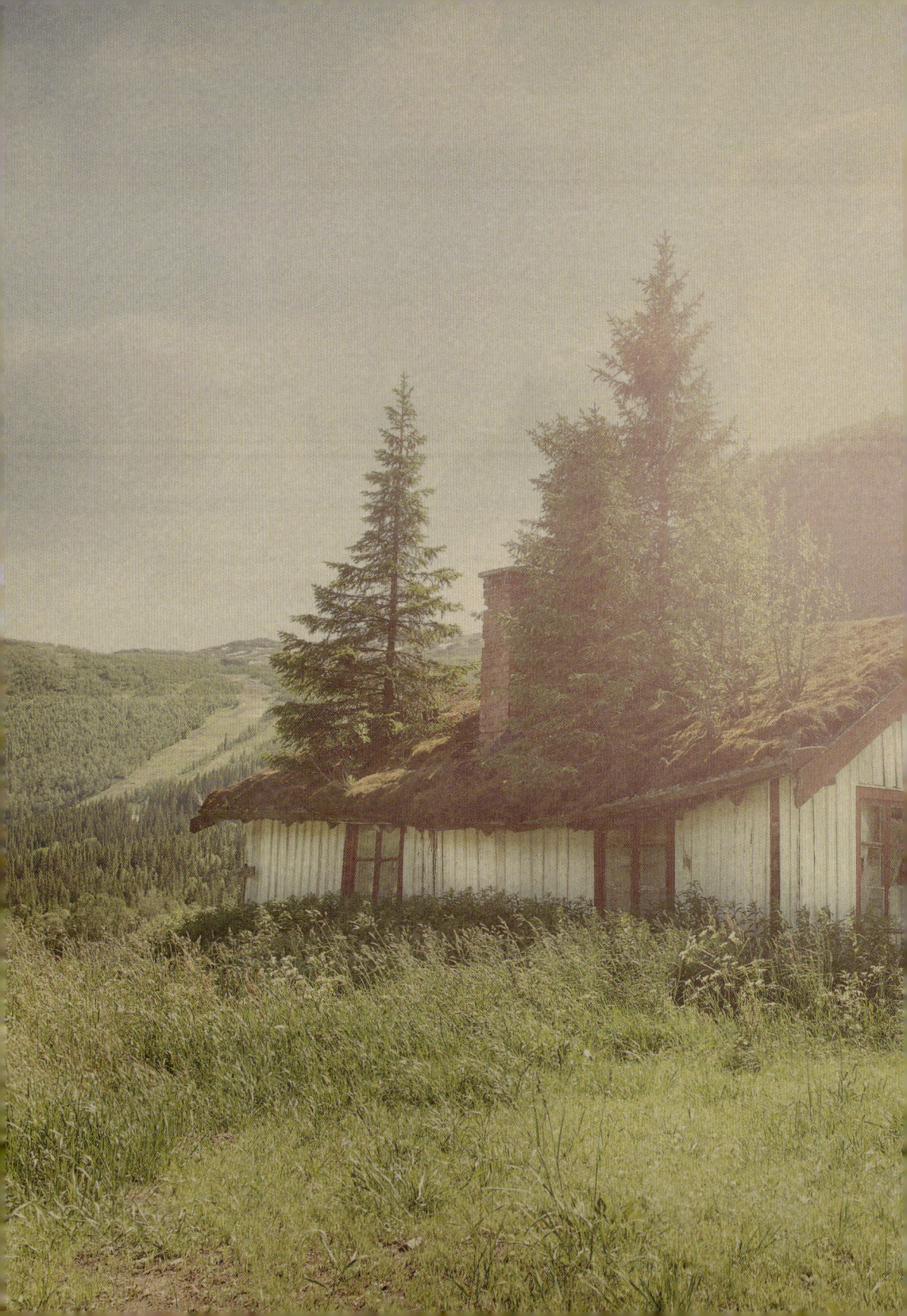

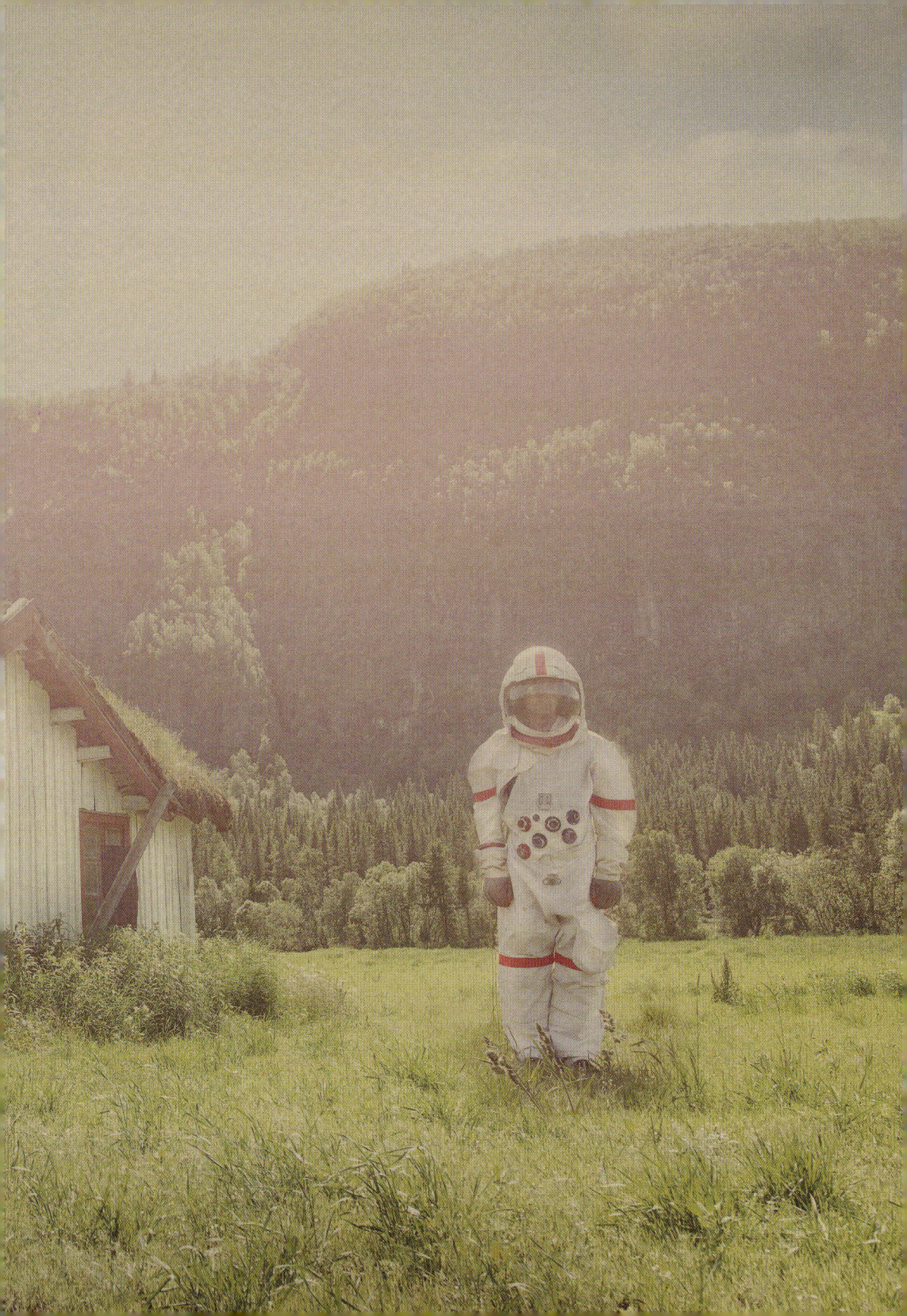

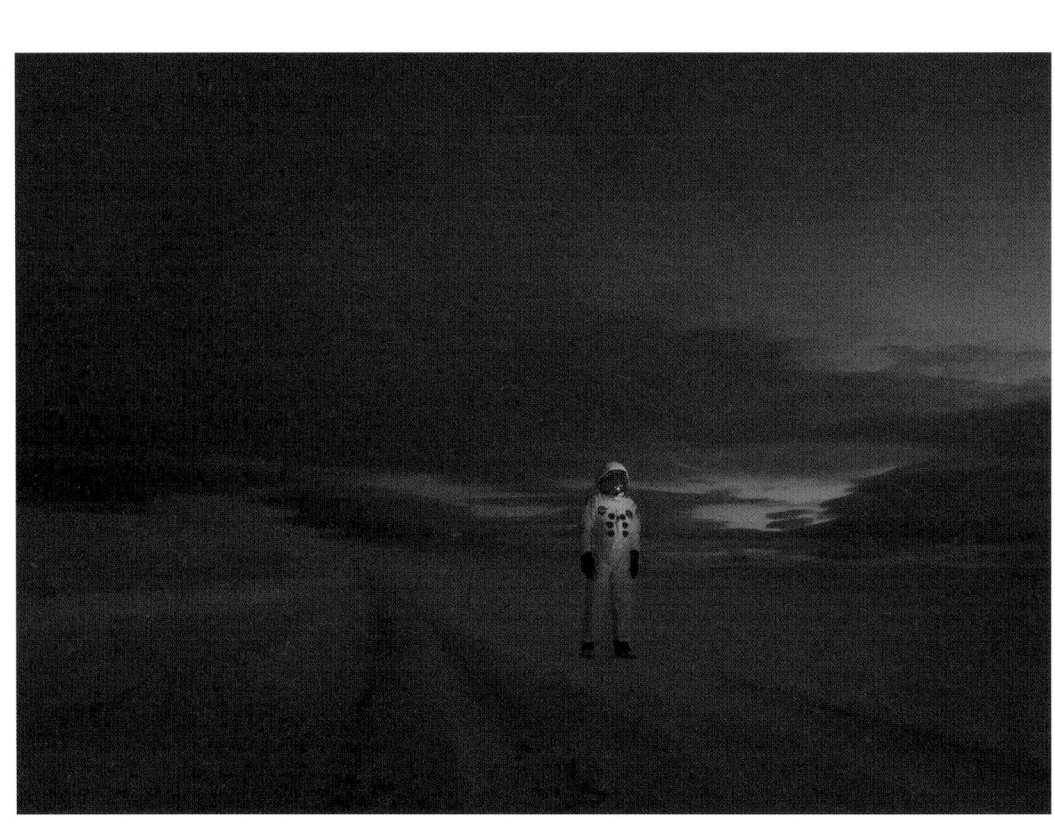

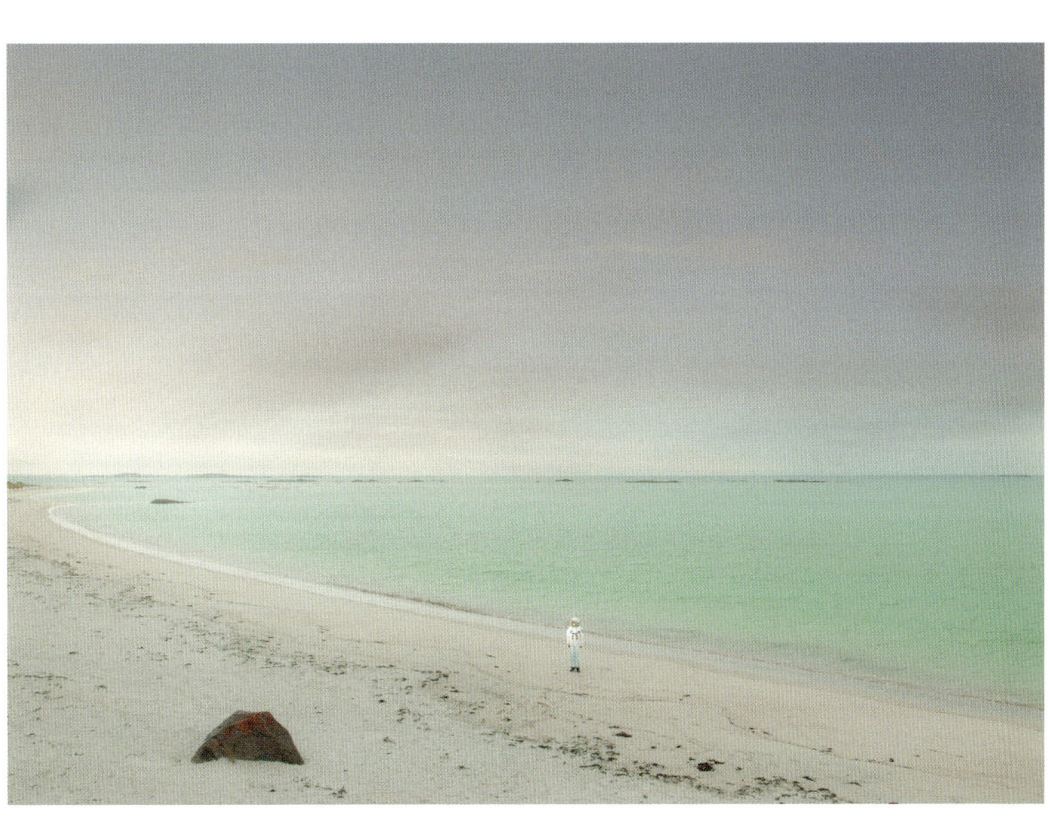

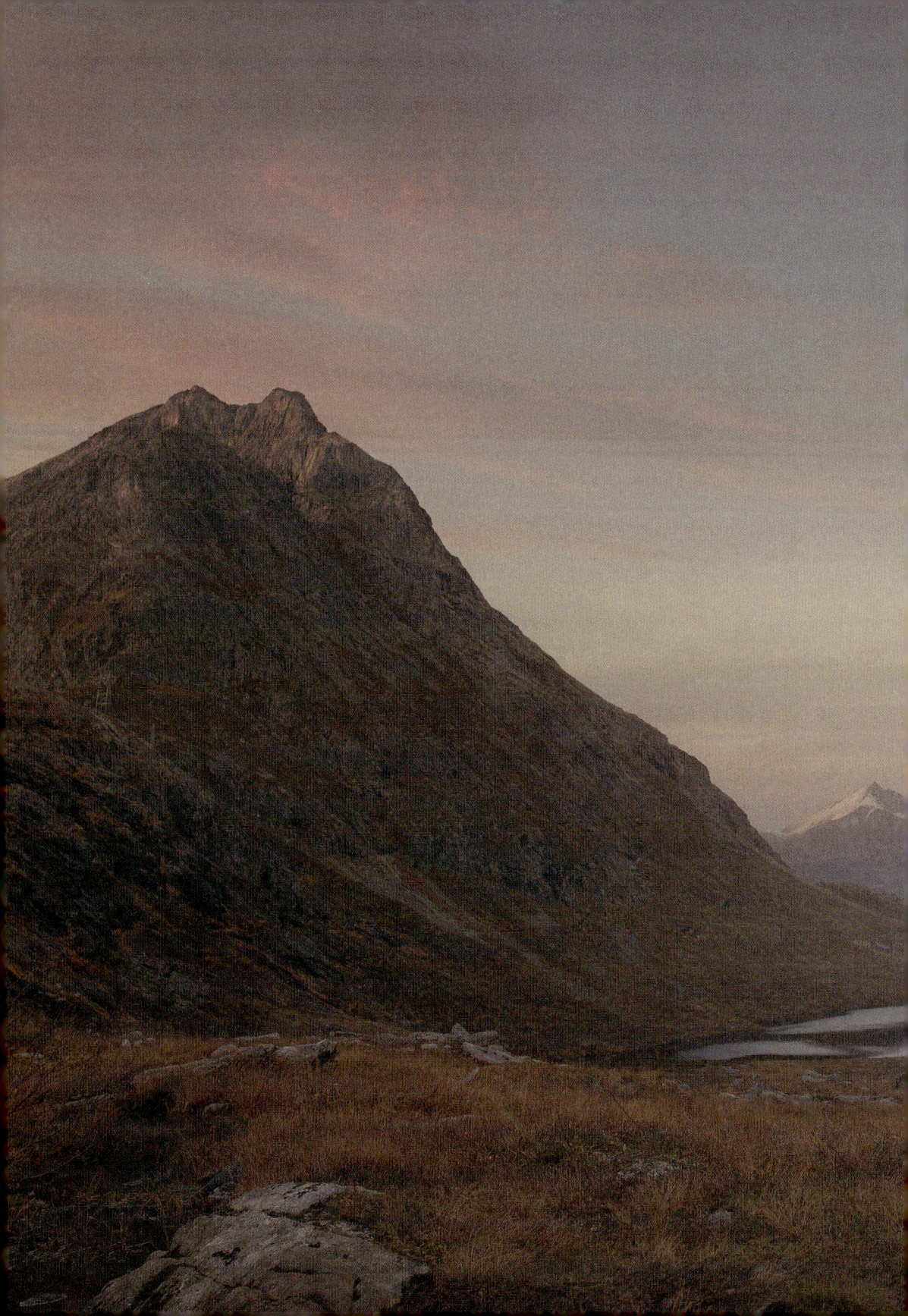

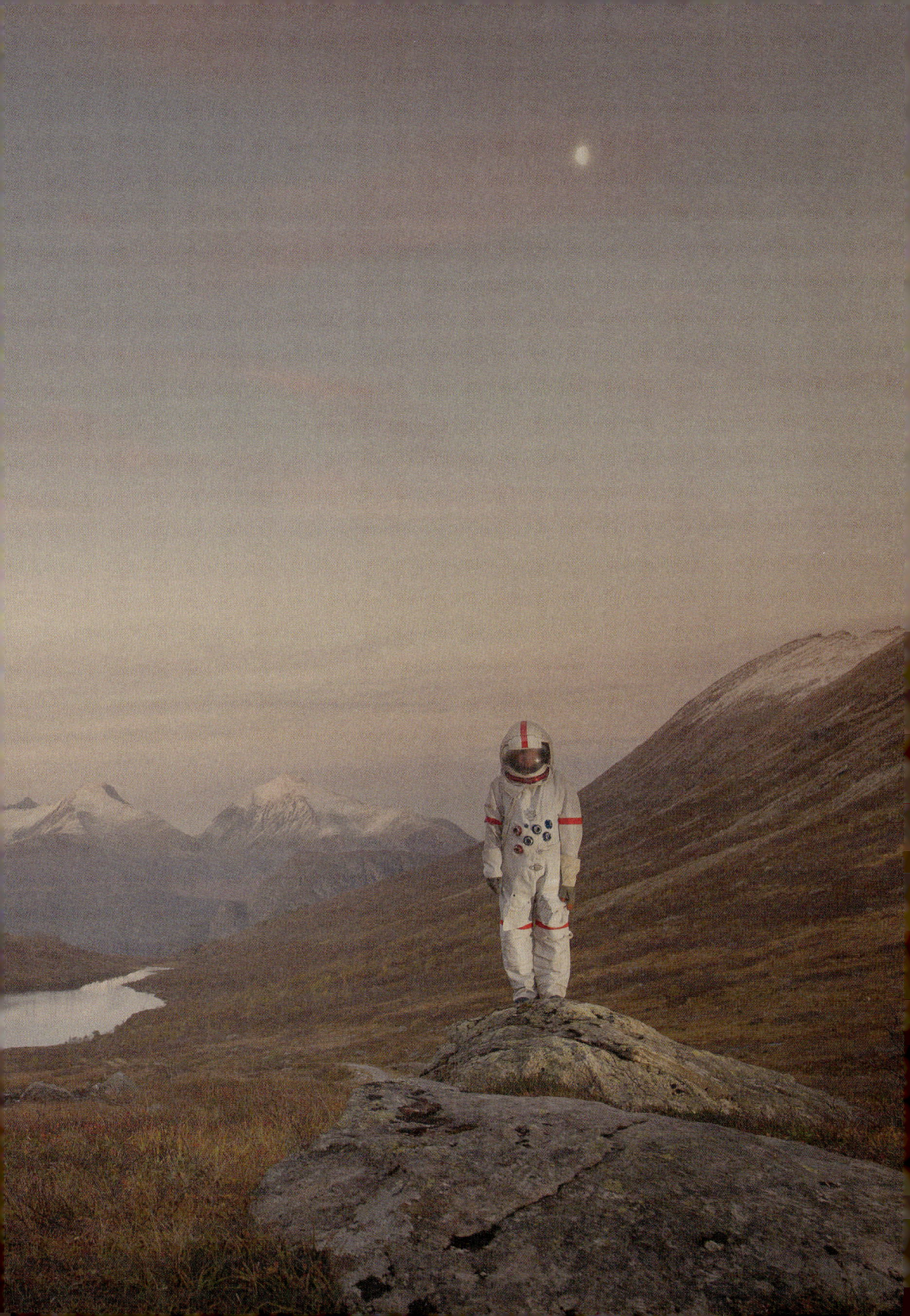

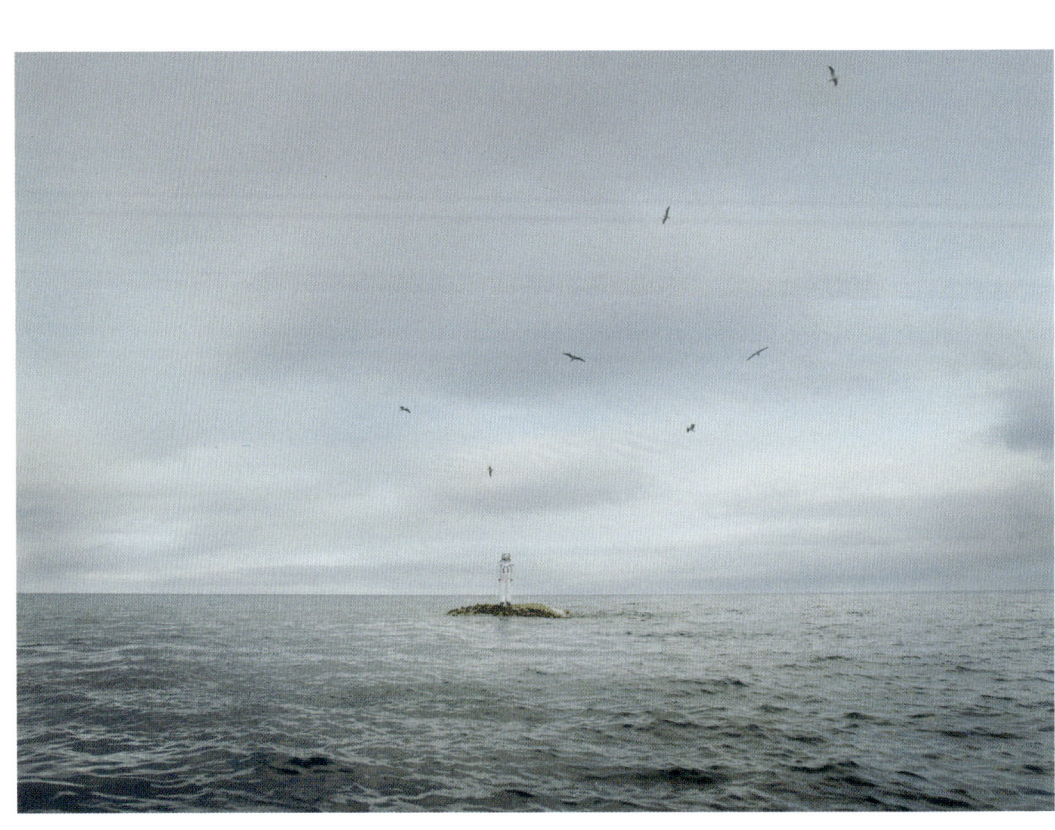

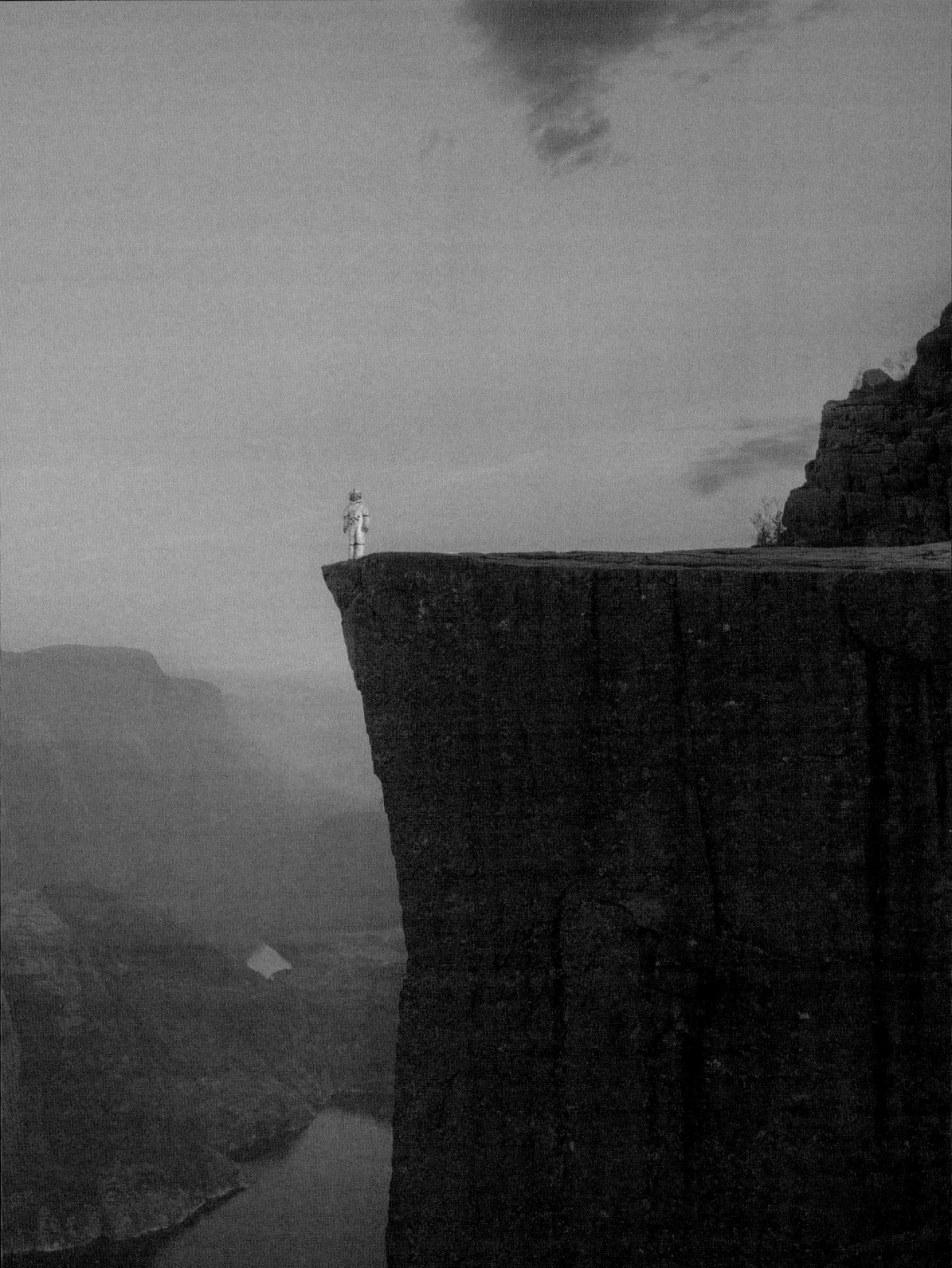

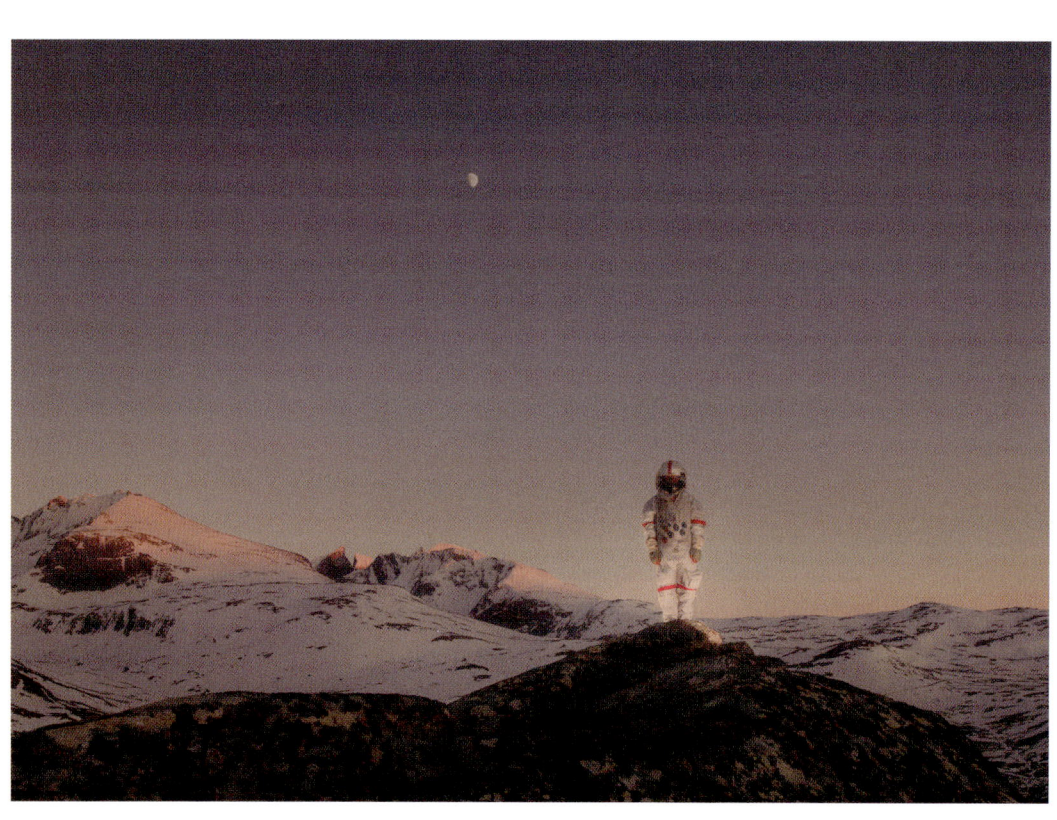

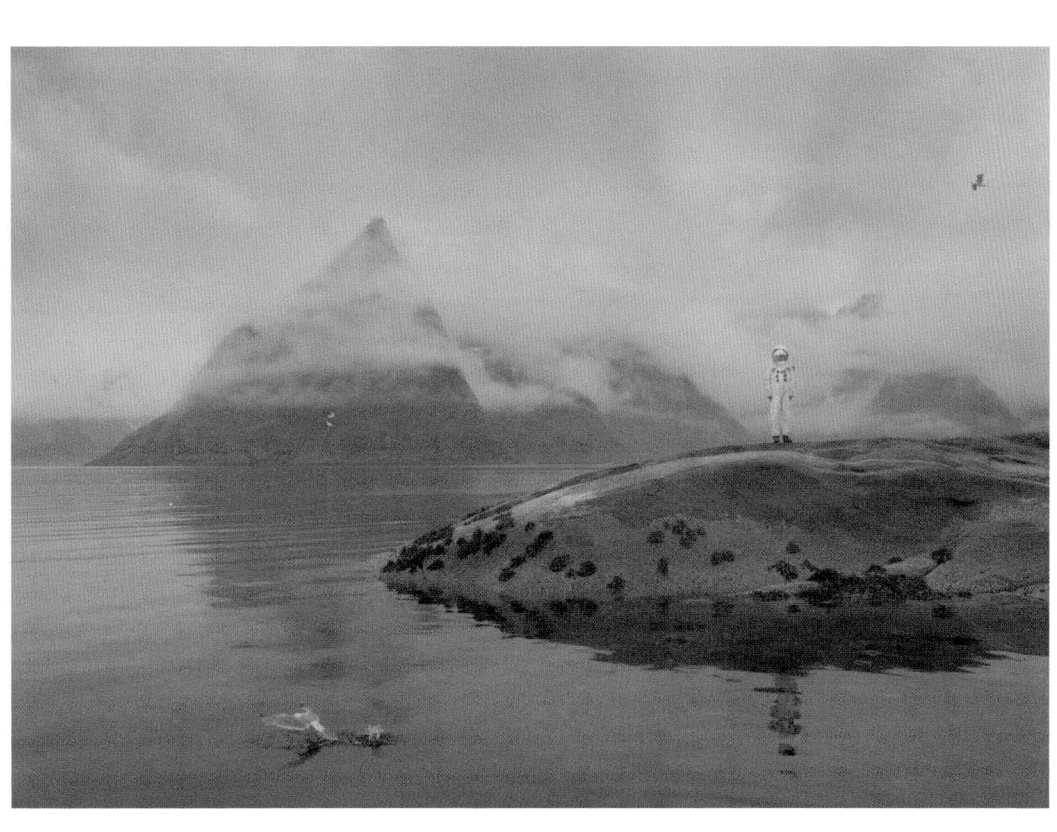

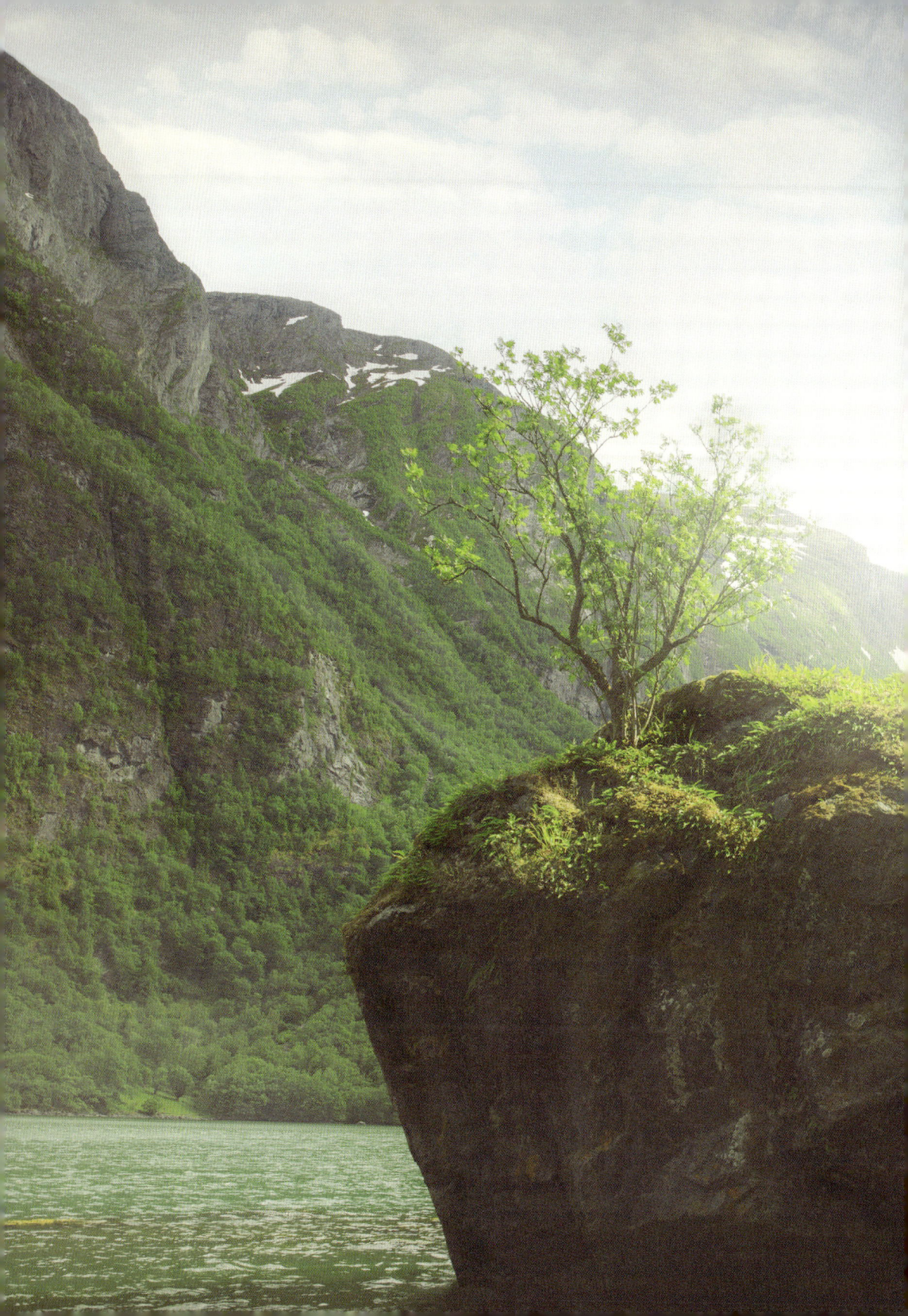

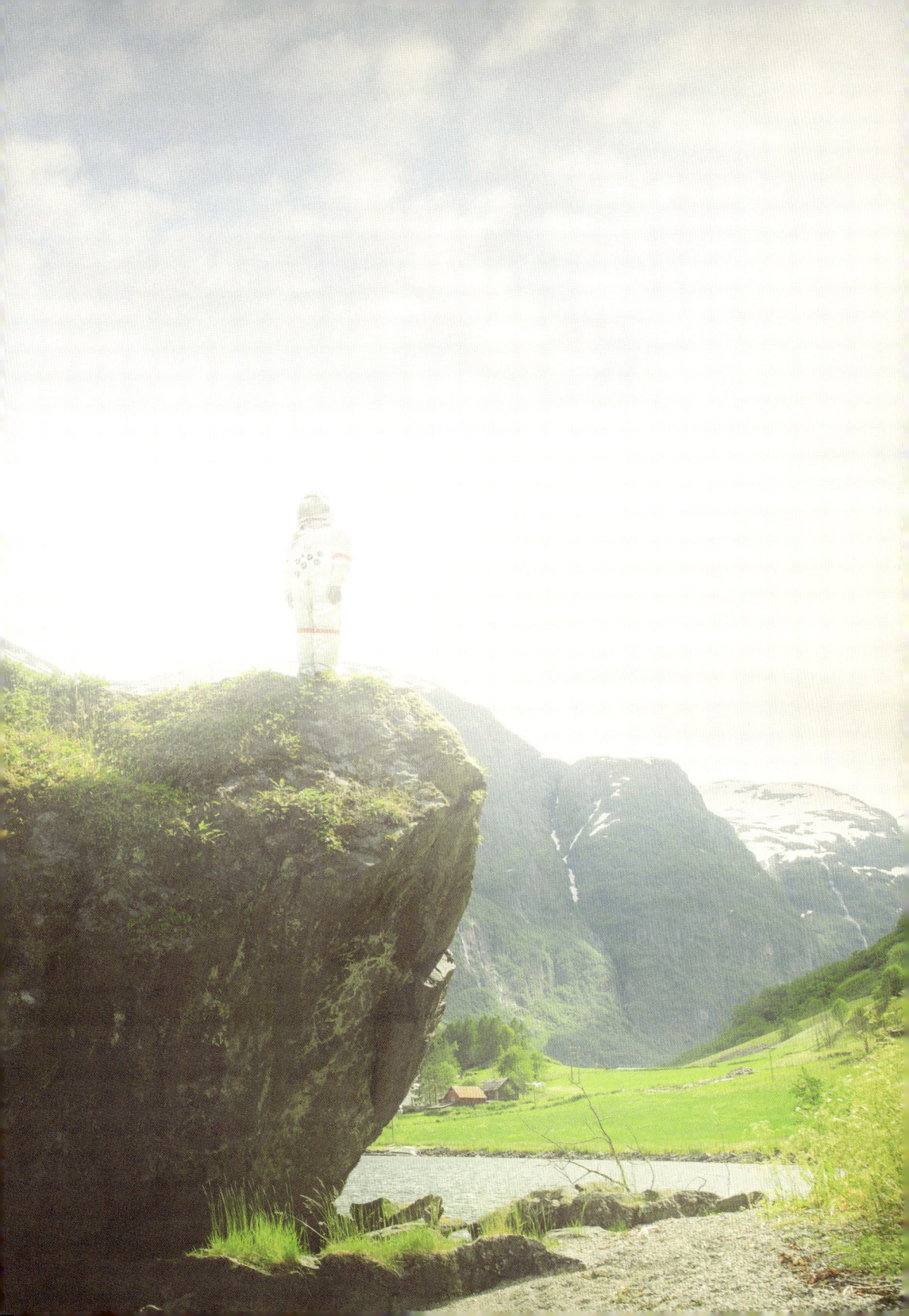

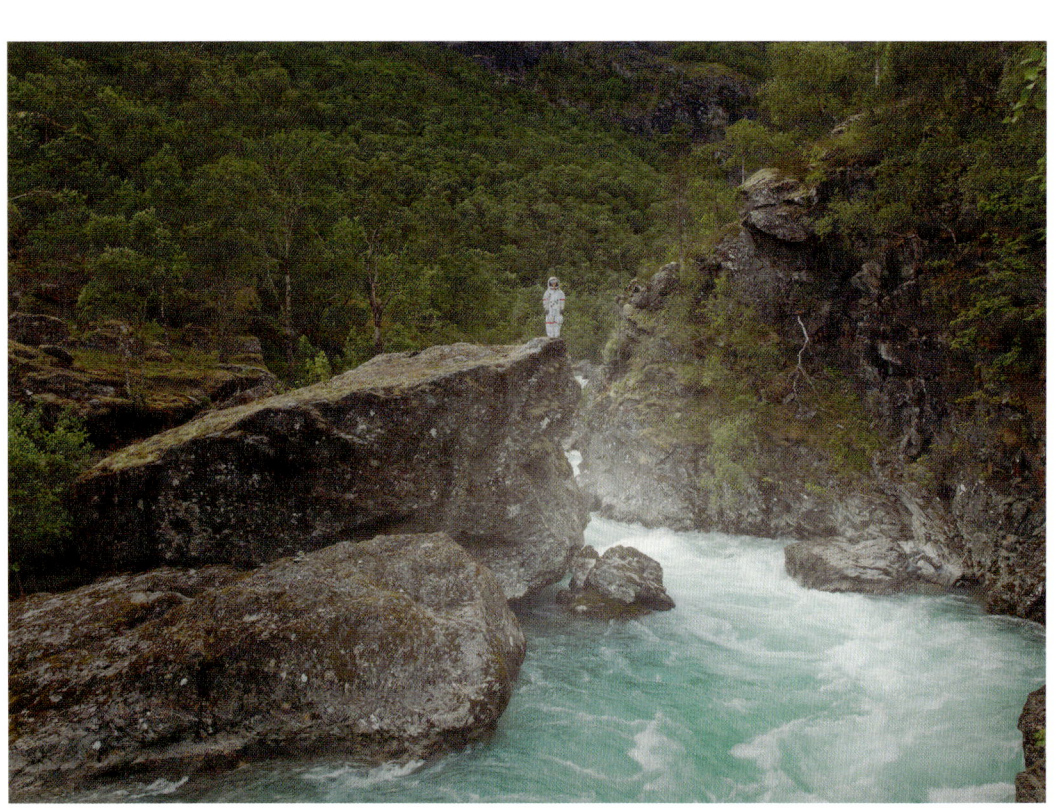

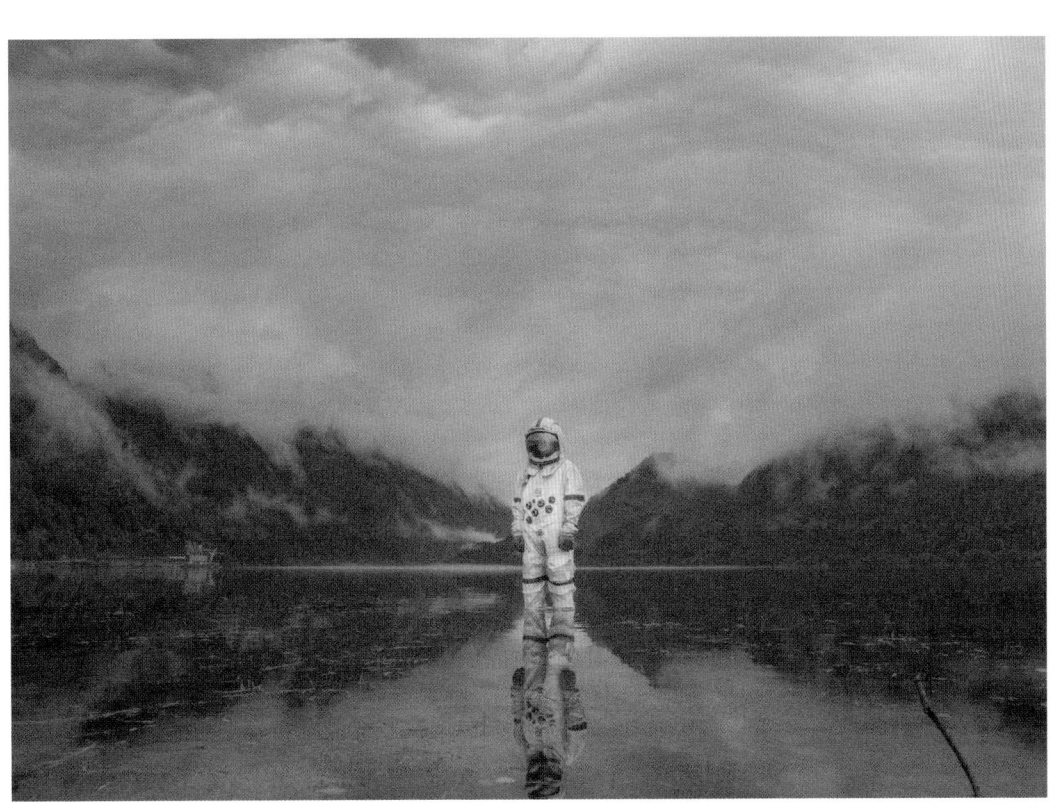

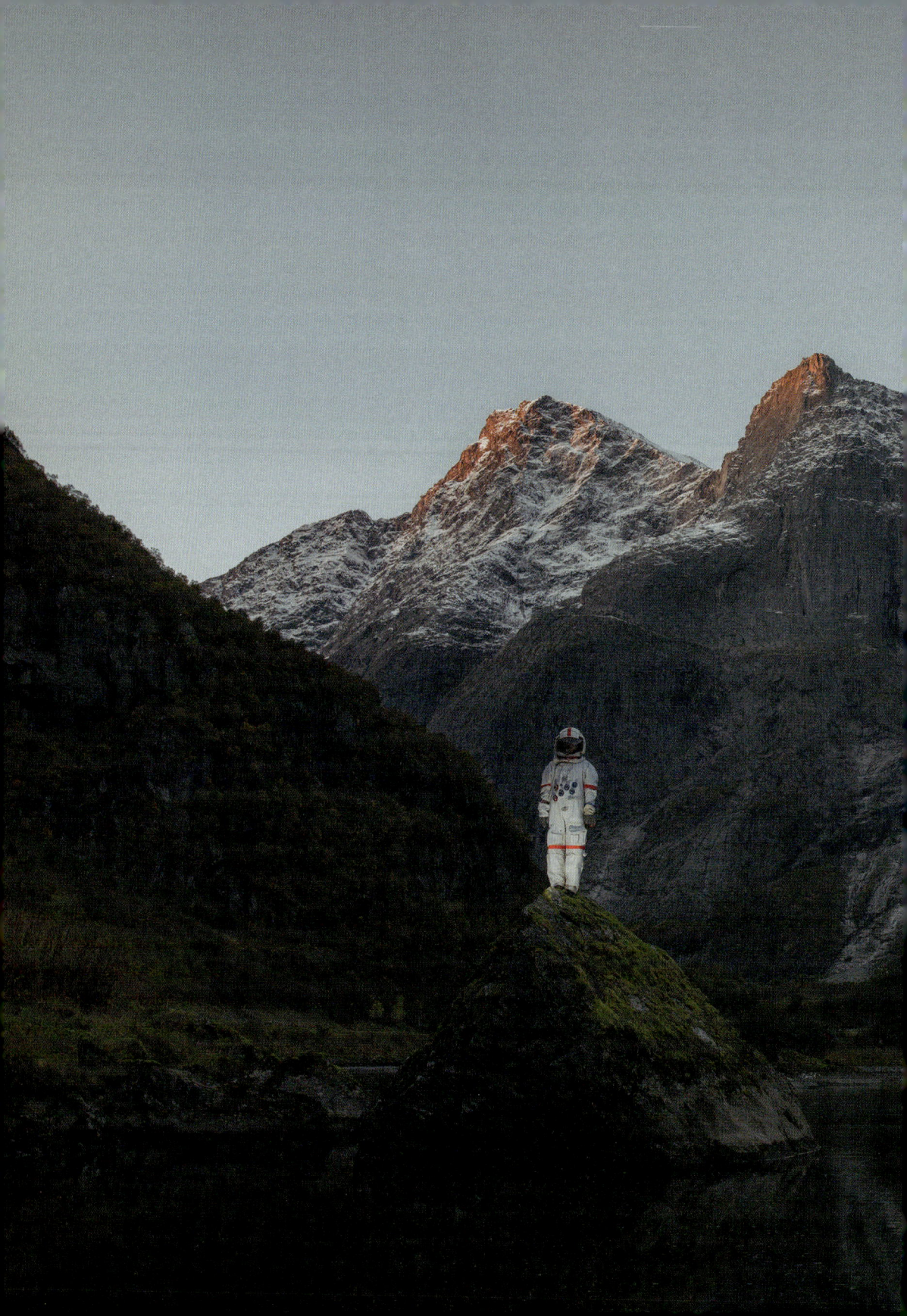

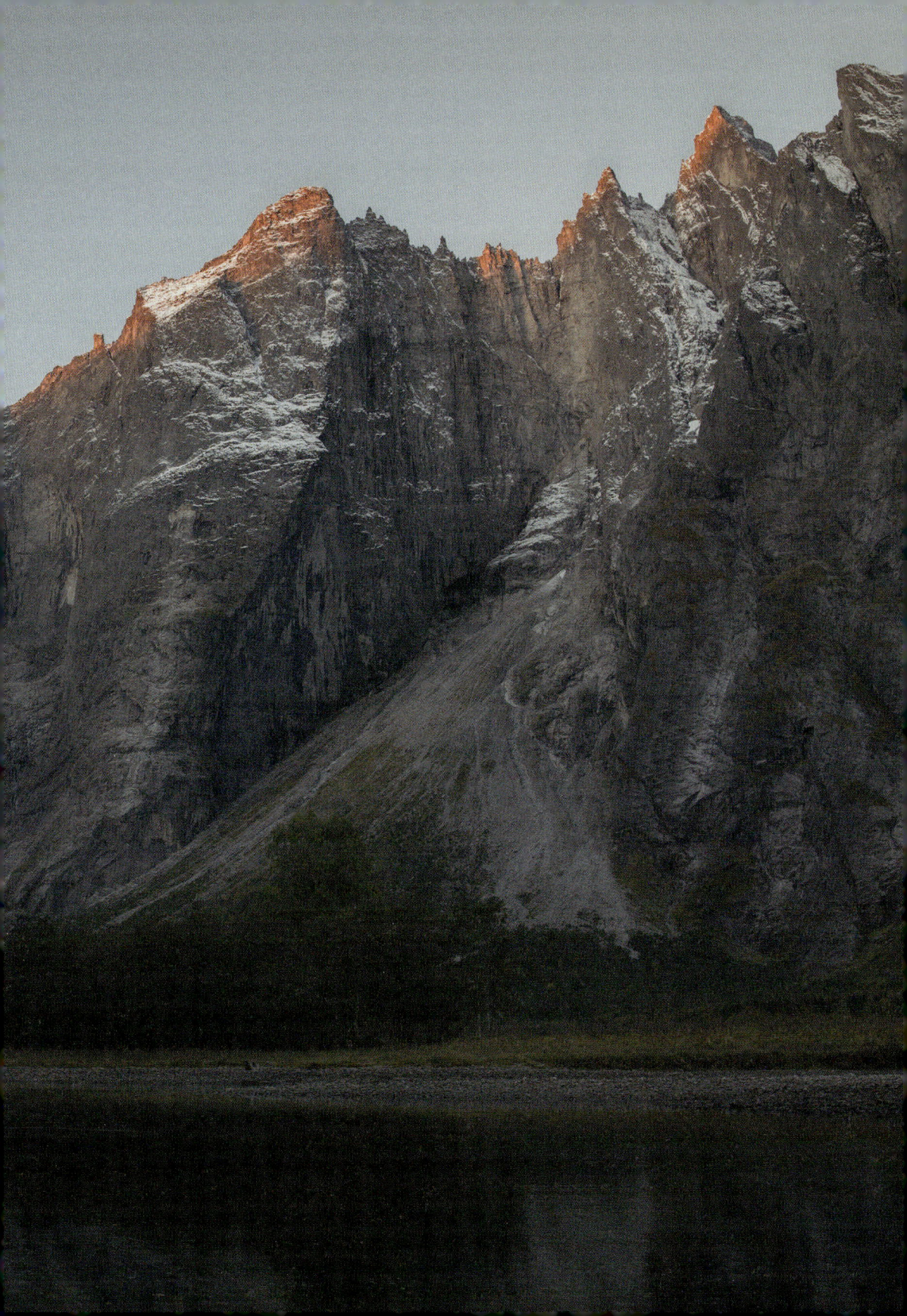

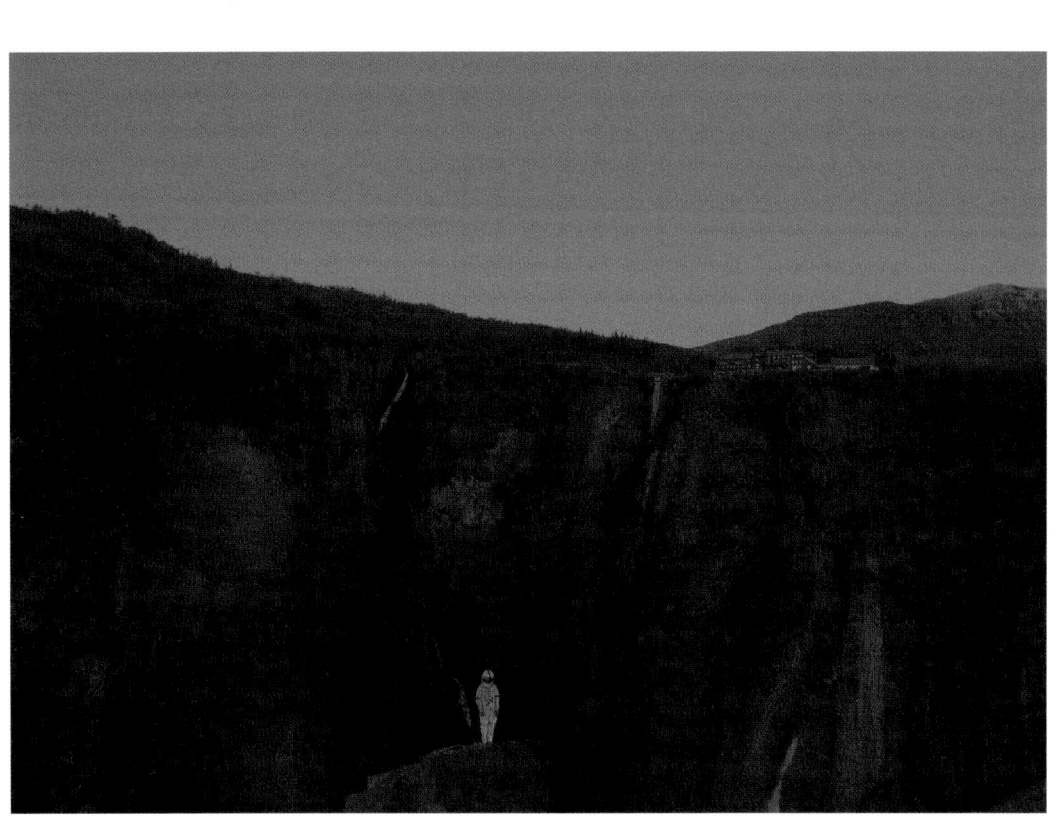

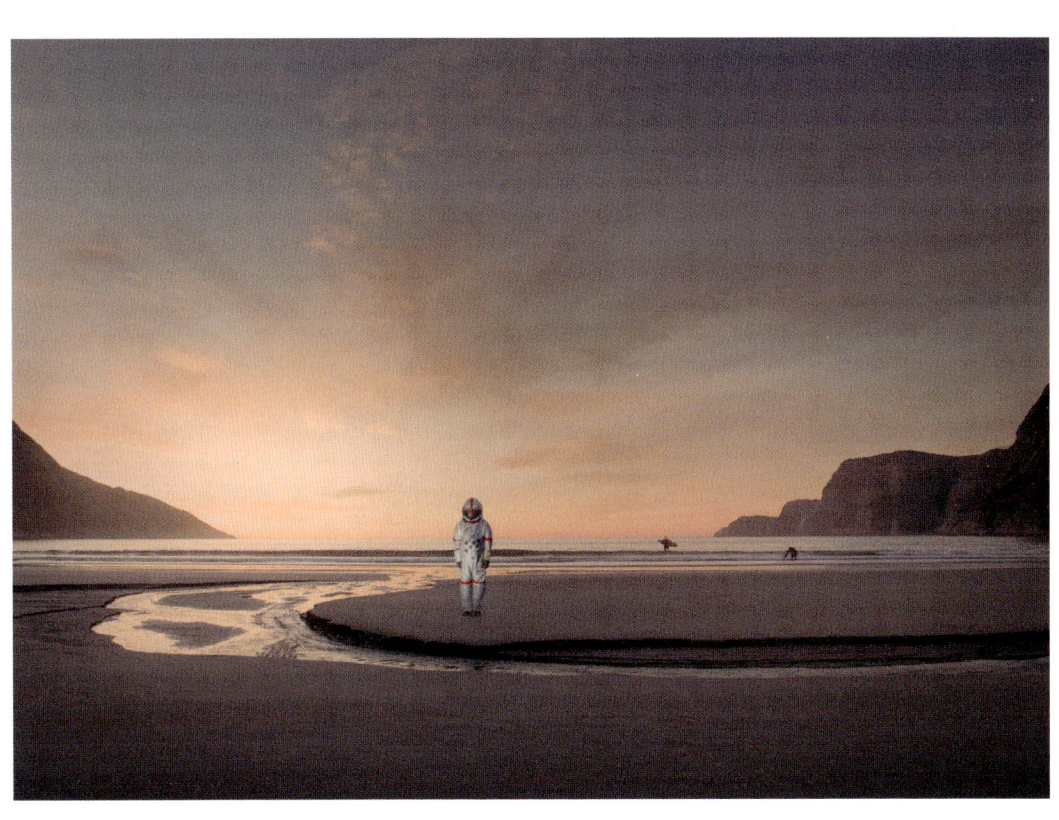

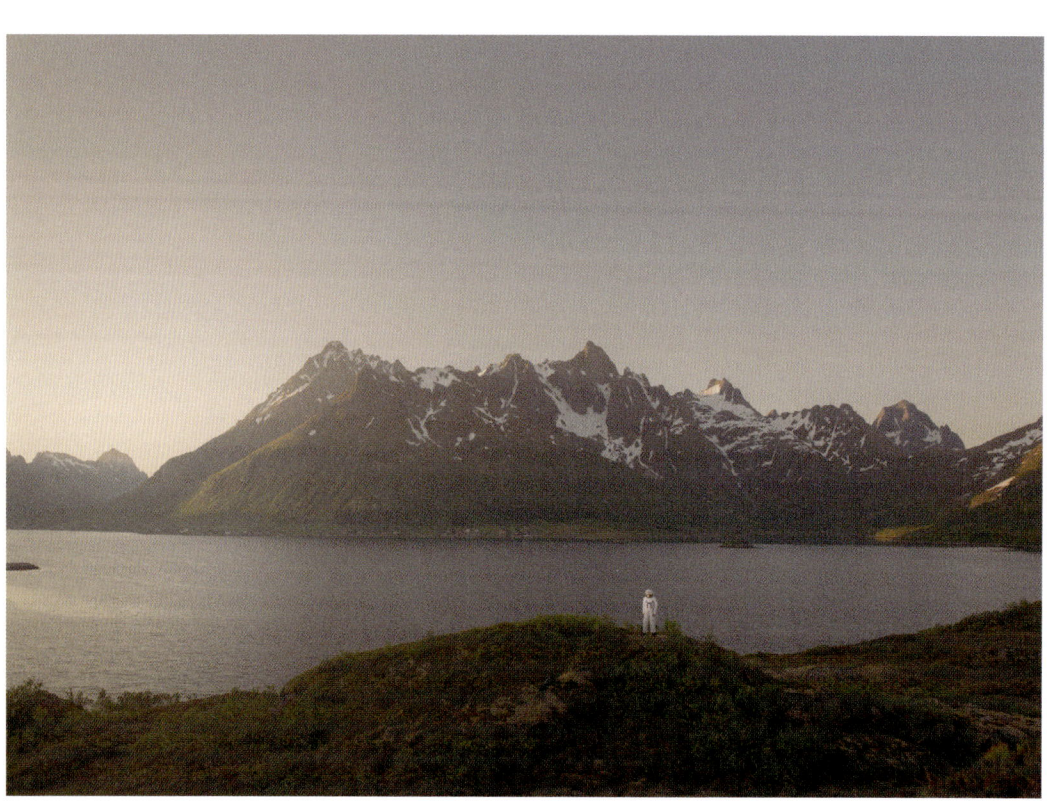

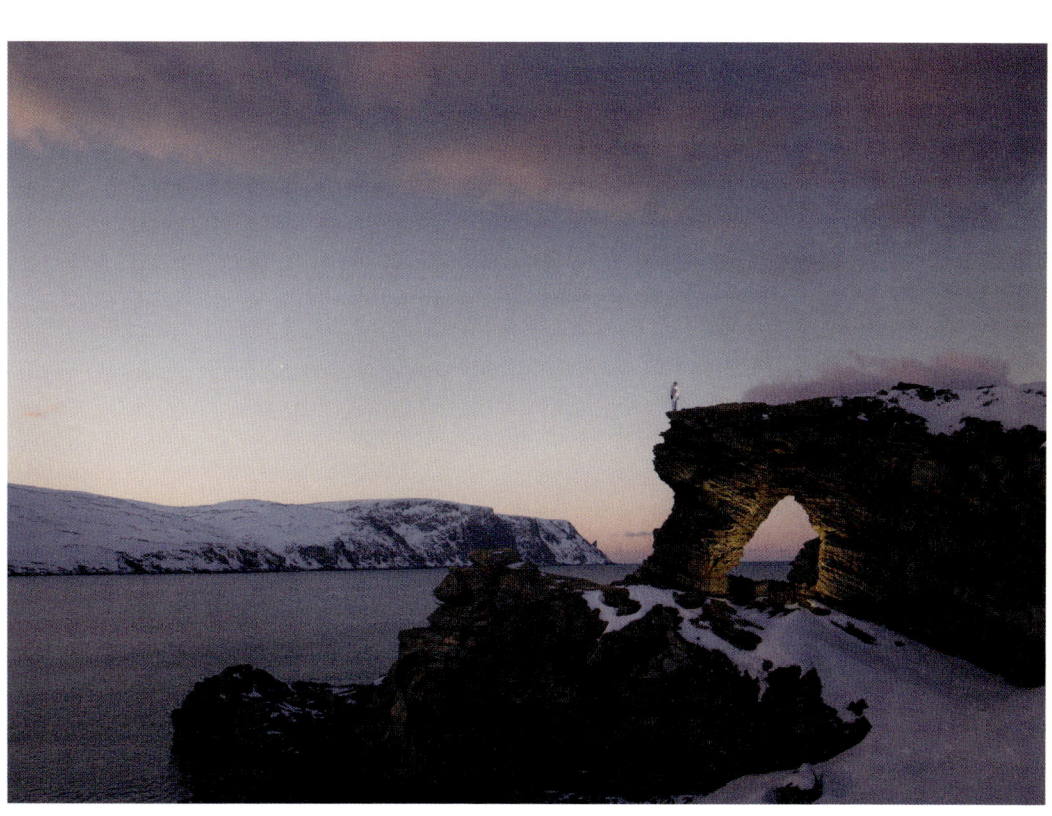

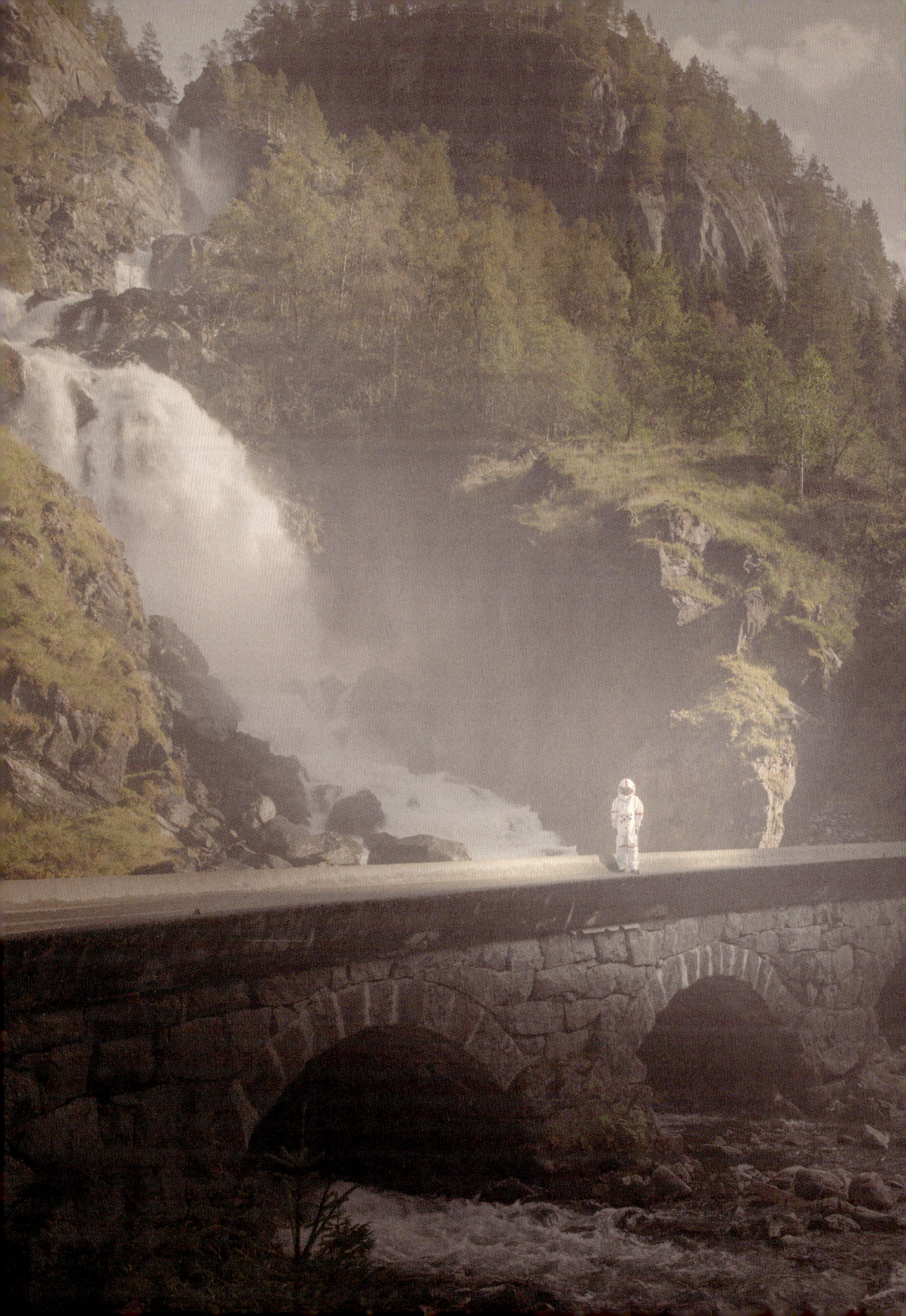

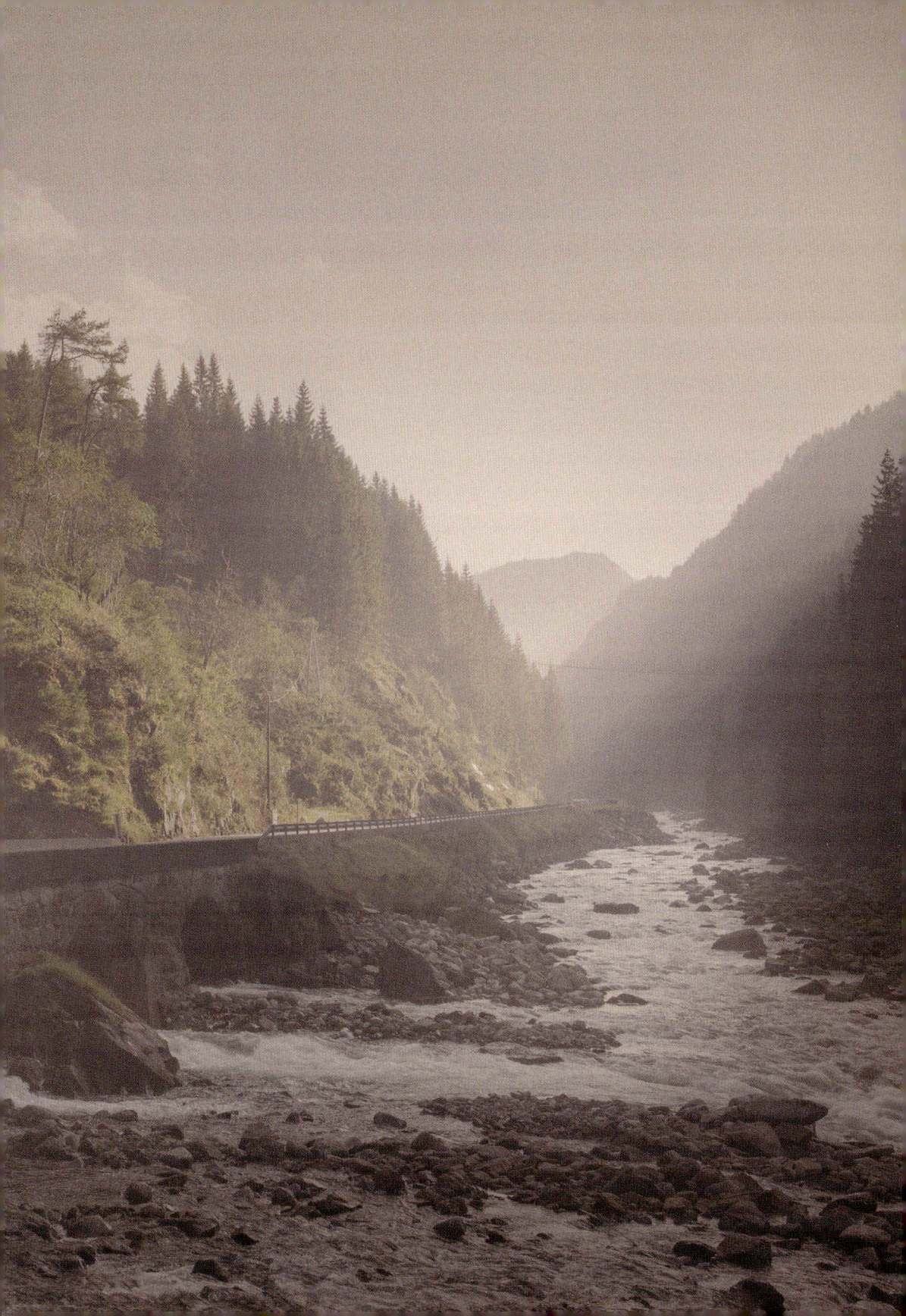

VIGNETTES OF A SALESMAN

2016–2018

"Vignettes of a Salesman", from 2016, is a love letter to simpler times of Scandinavia in the 1950s and 1960s as we follow a lonely, faceless salesman on his never-ending rounds knocking on doors.

A relic of the 50s that has now disappeared, the series follows the main character on a silent, solitary journey – a figure from the past in the modern world.

Like the fictional character, Willy Loman, from Arthur Miller's 'Death of a Salesman', the character and narrative are driven by the search for identity and a place in the modern world. Just as Miller based his character on his own uncle, Joergensen assigned the role of his nameless salesman to his uncle who

played the part impeccably and helped out on the set.

Shot exclusively in the sparsely populated areas of rural Norway, the dominant landscape becomes the "windows and bricks" that are closing in on the character in the latter years of his life.

The series reflects a life full of complex emotions, from the dark to the eccentric, associated with a stranger's life unfulfilled.

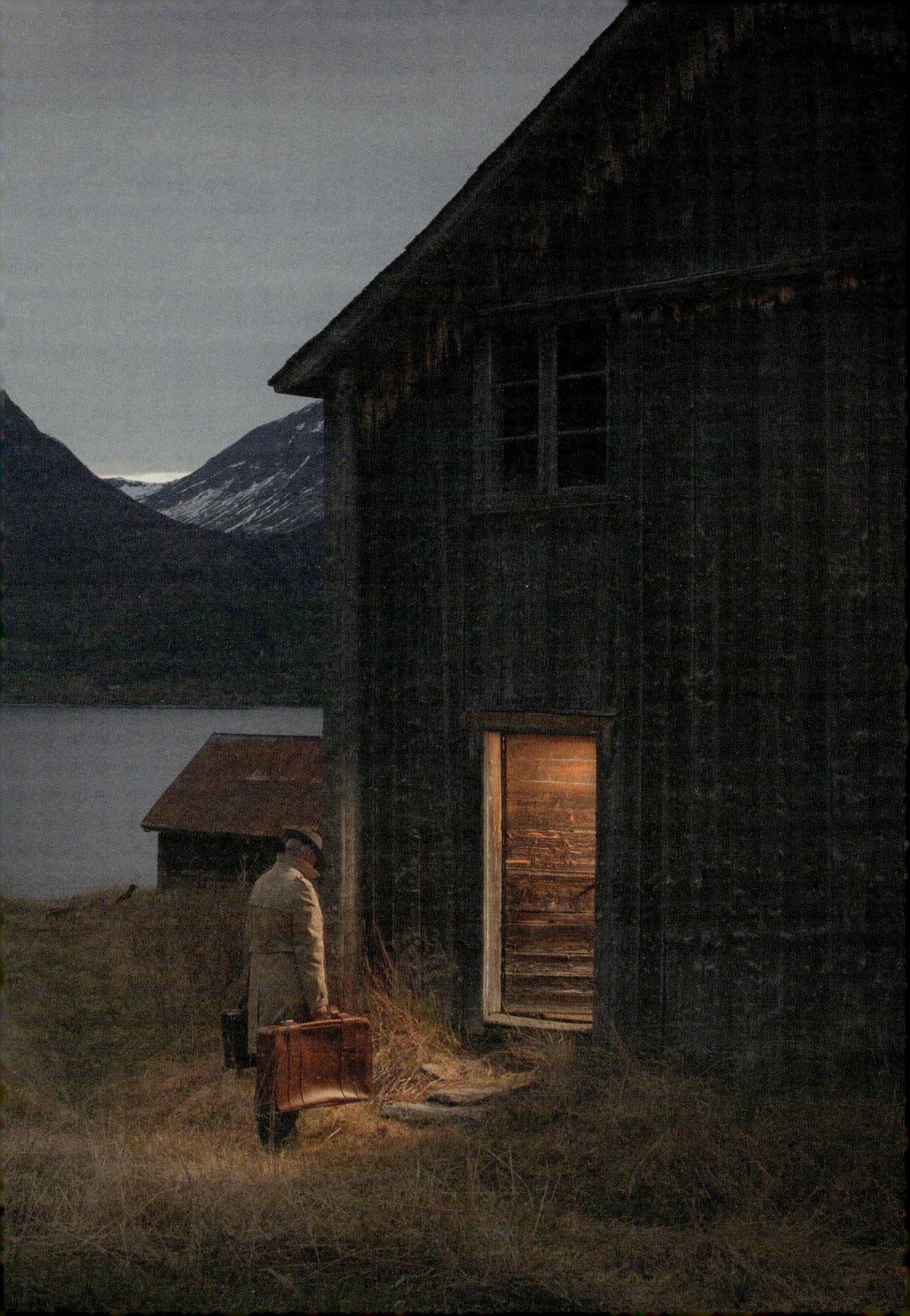

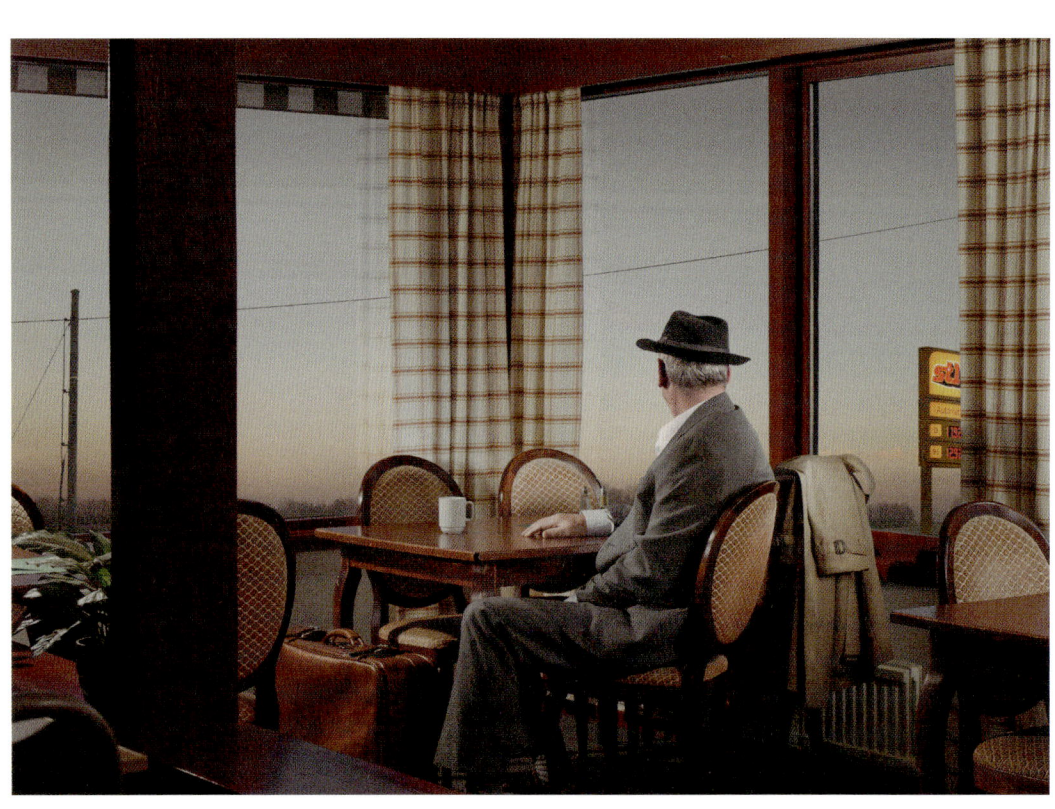

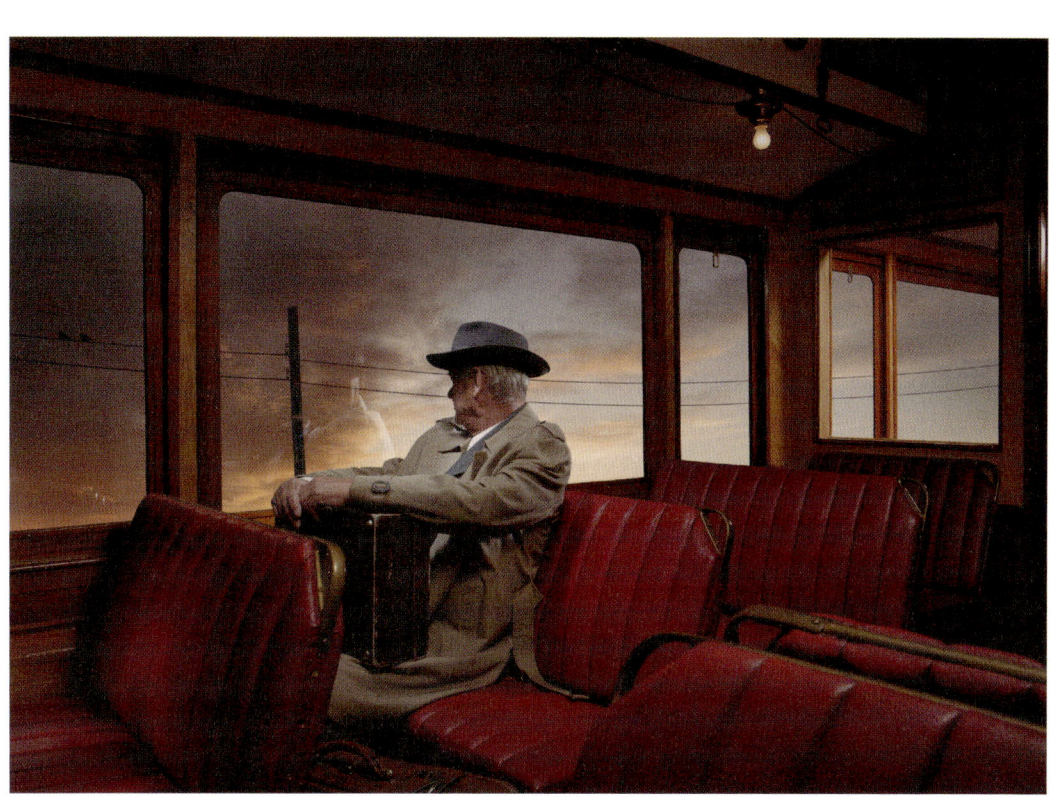

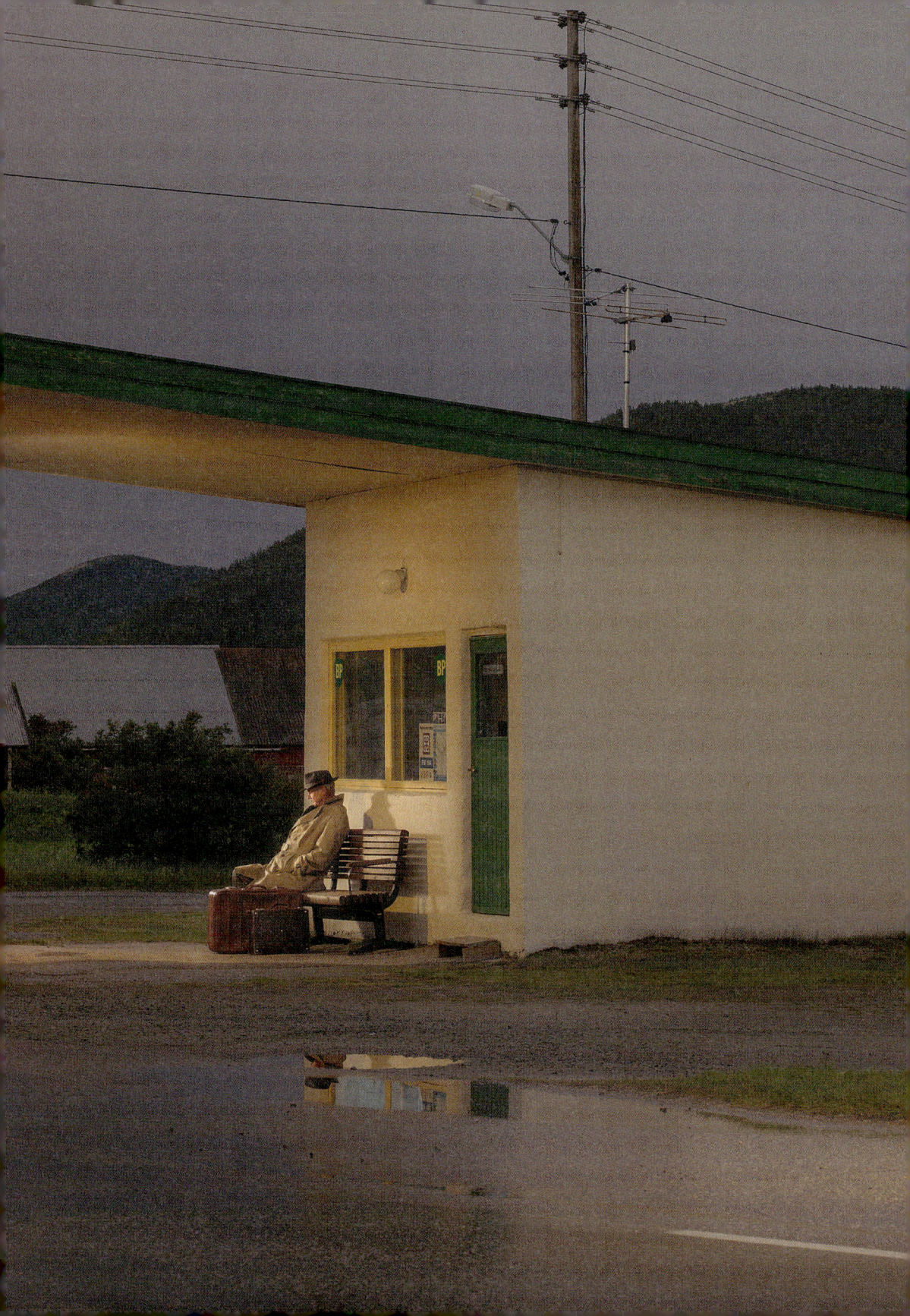

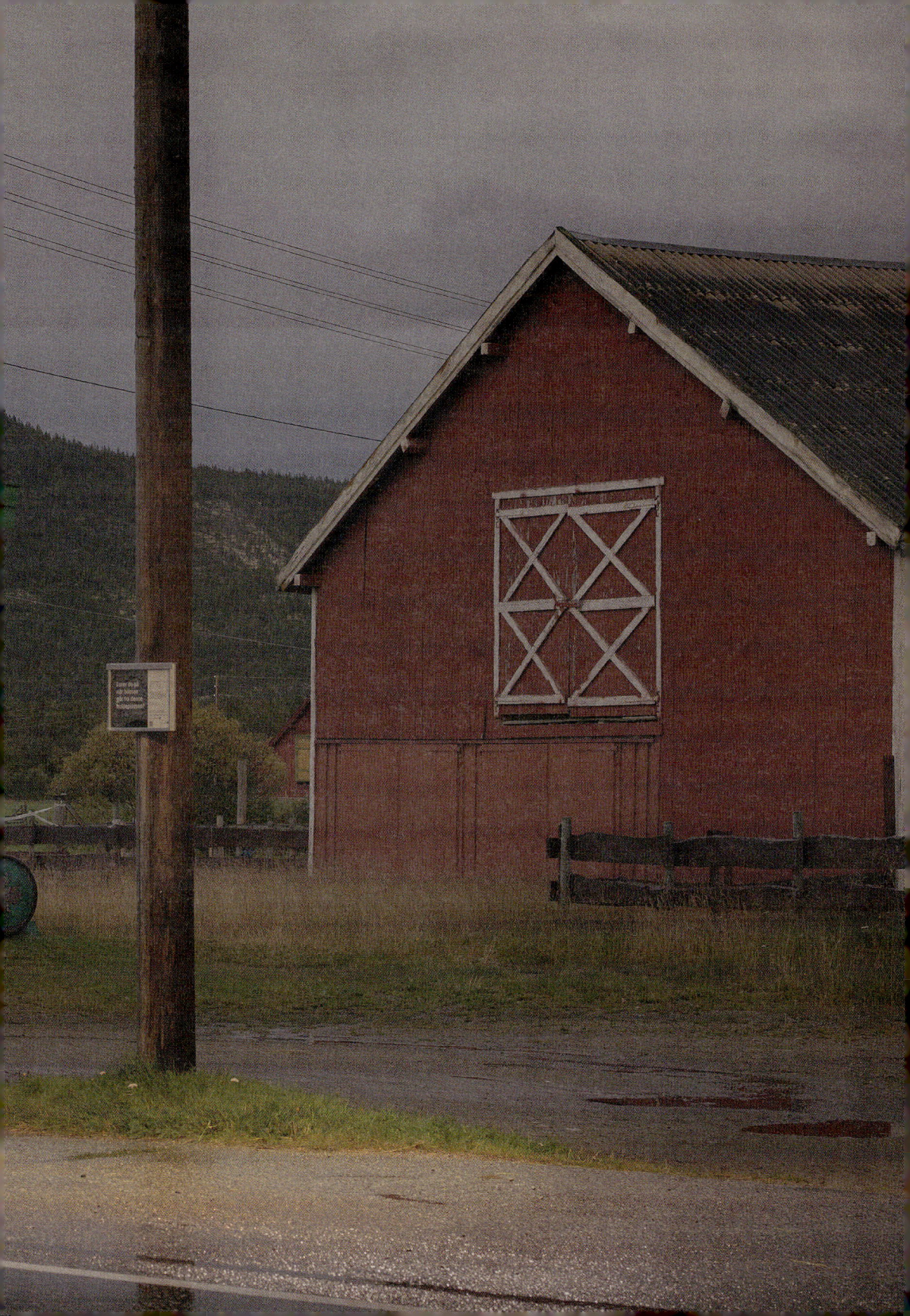

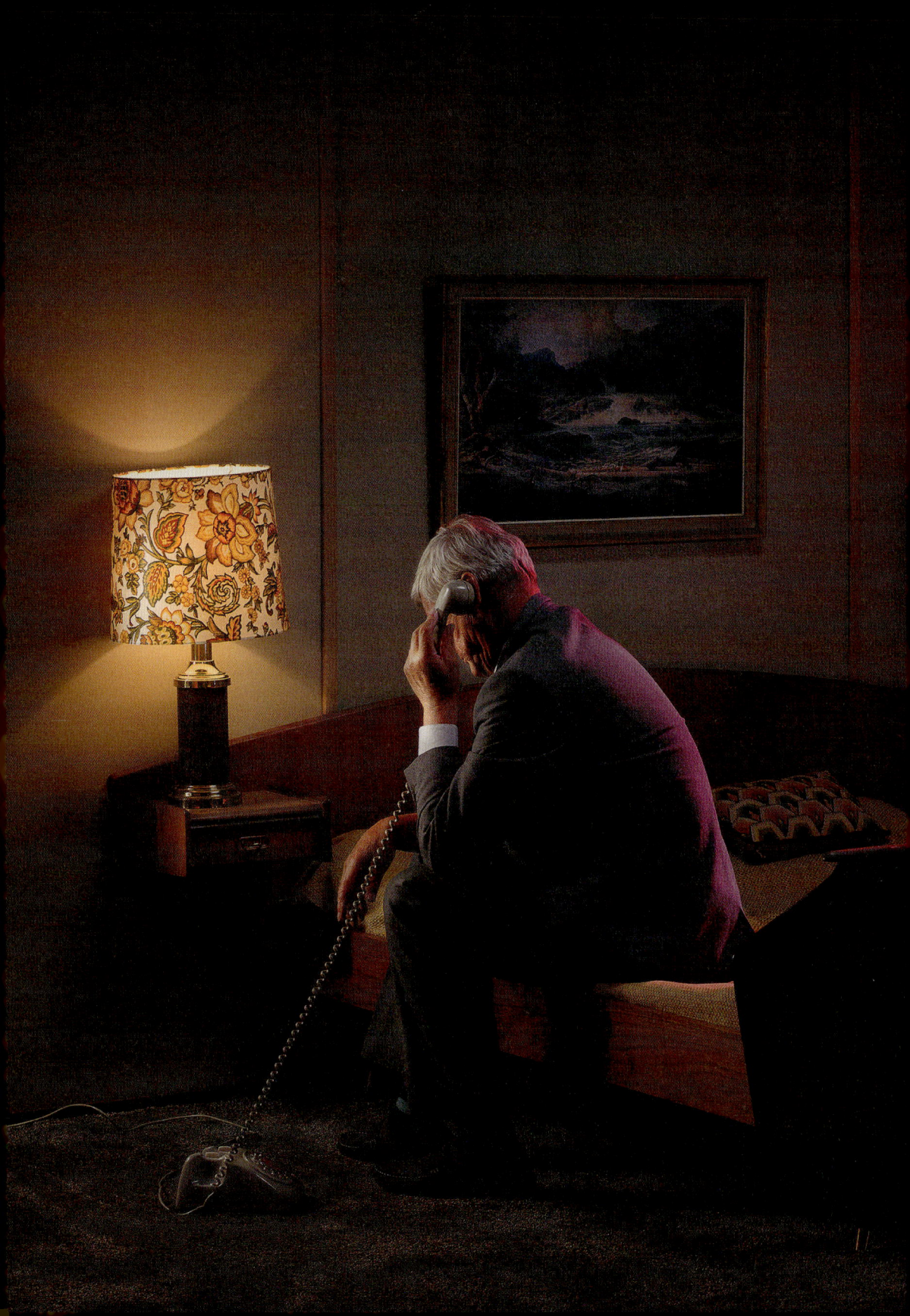

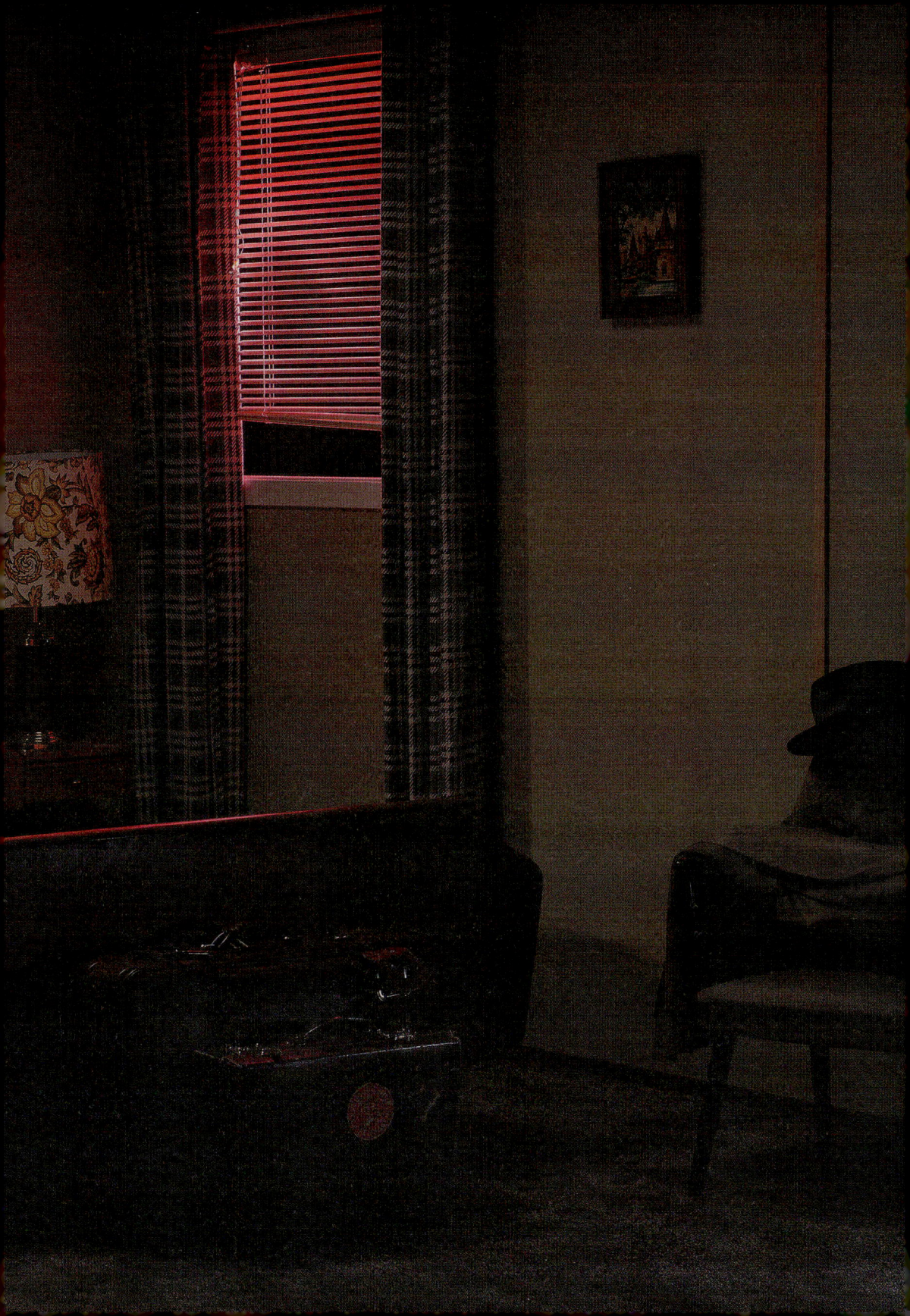

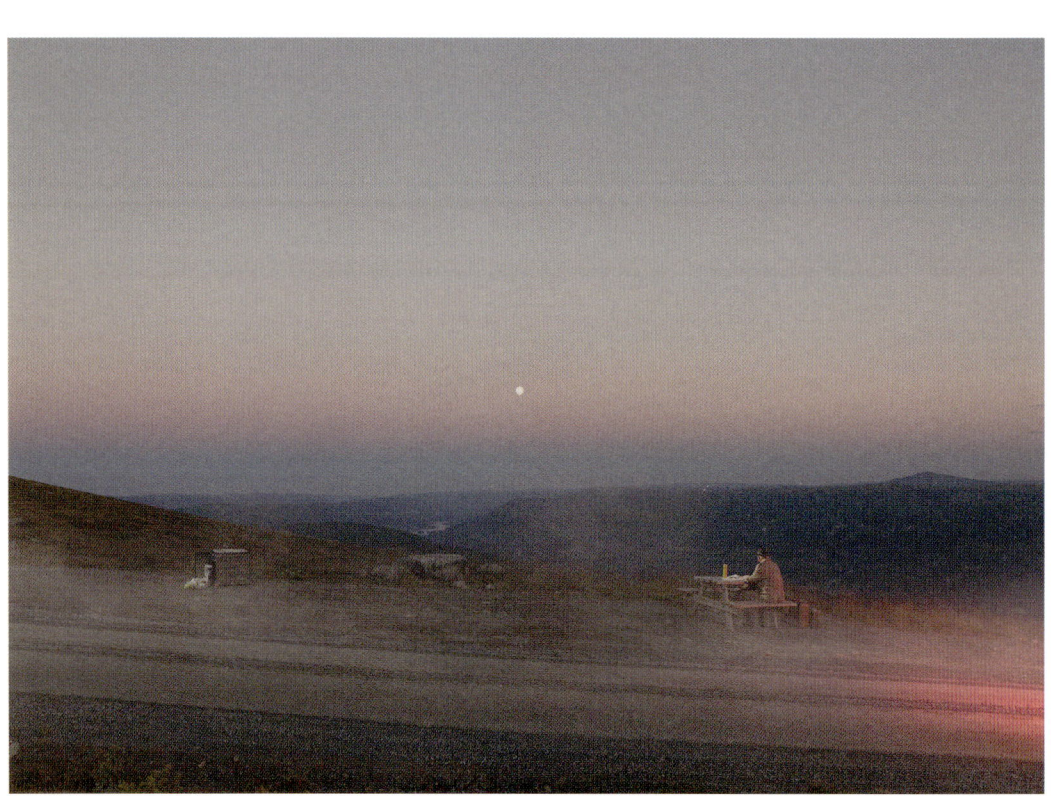

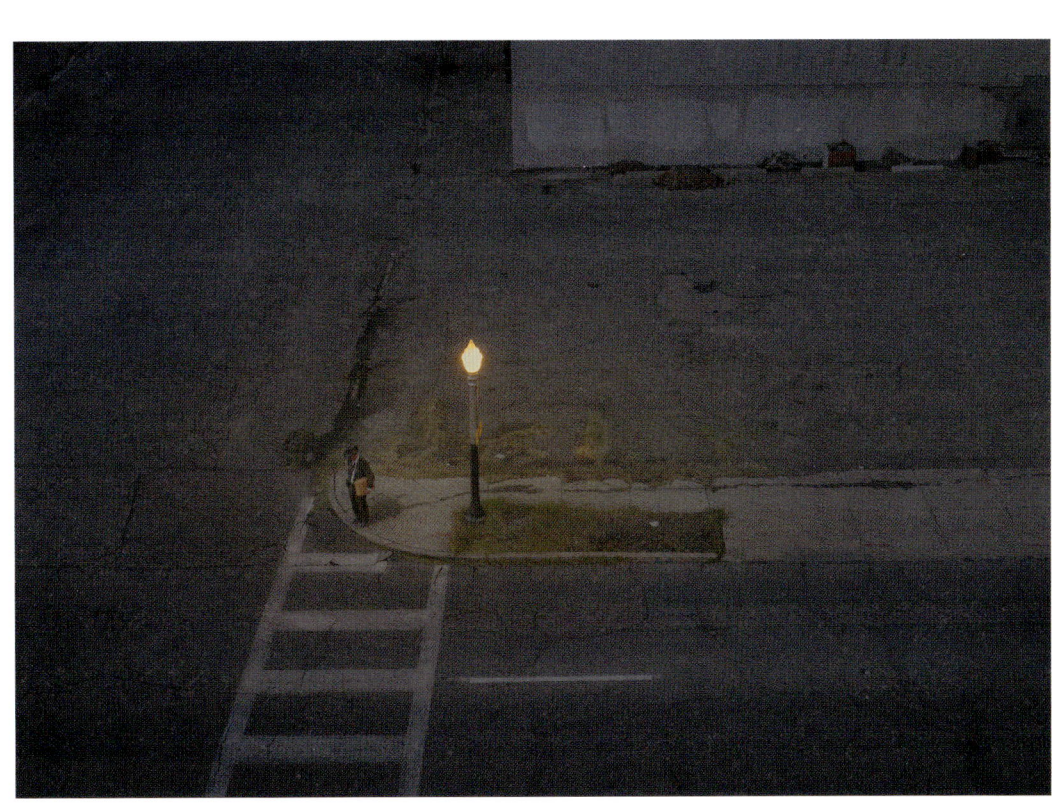

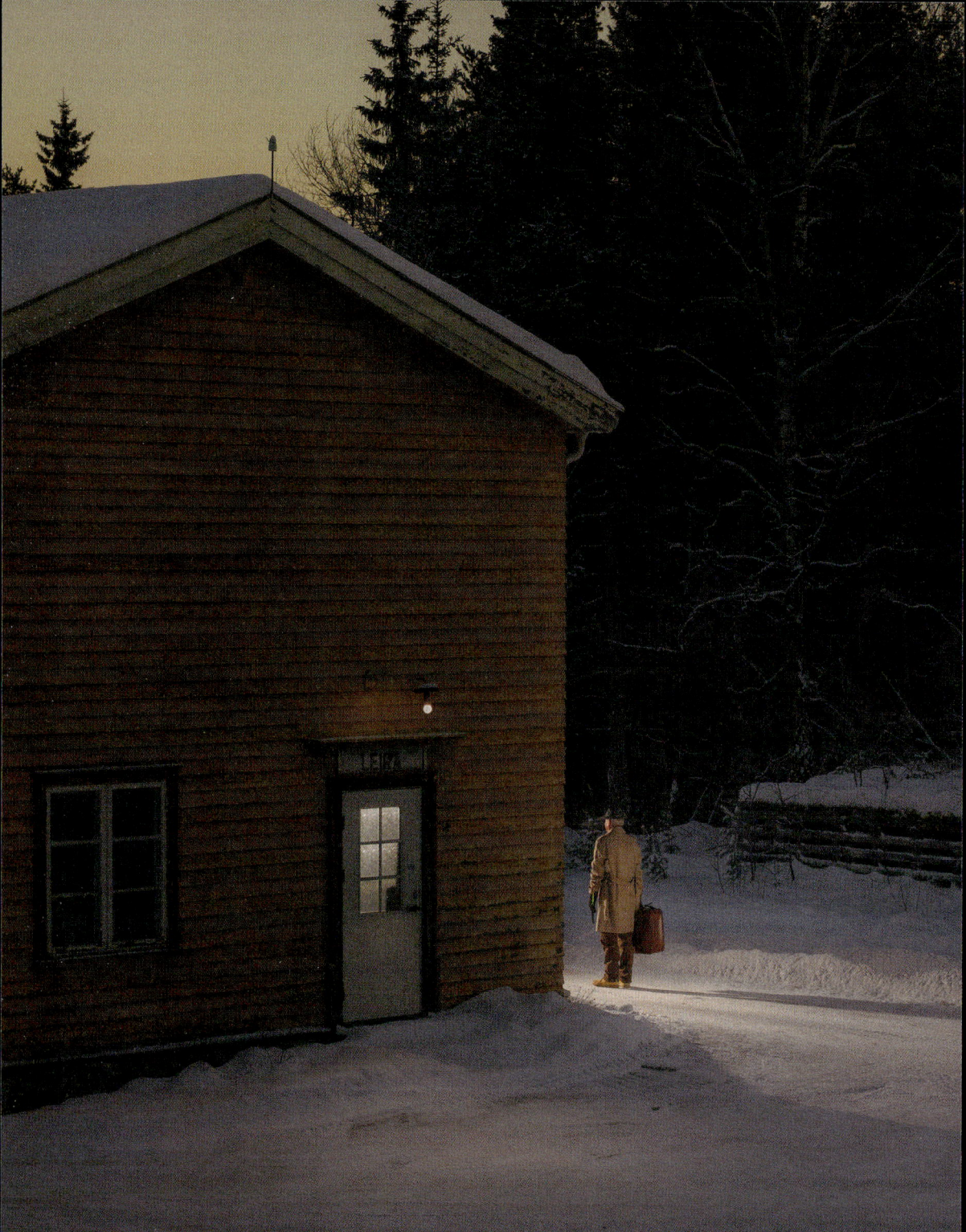

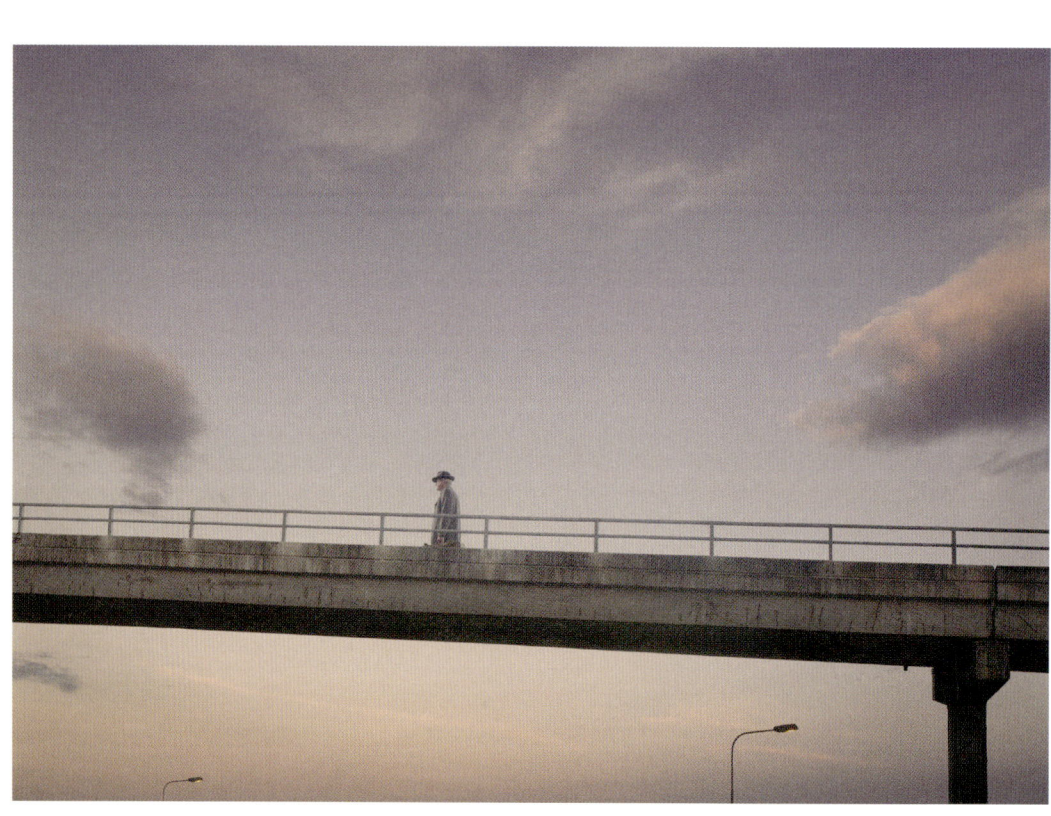

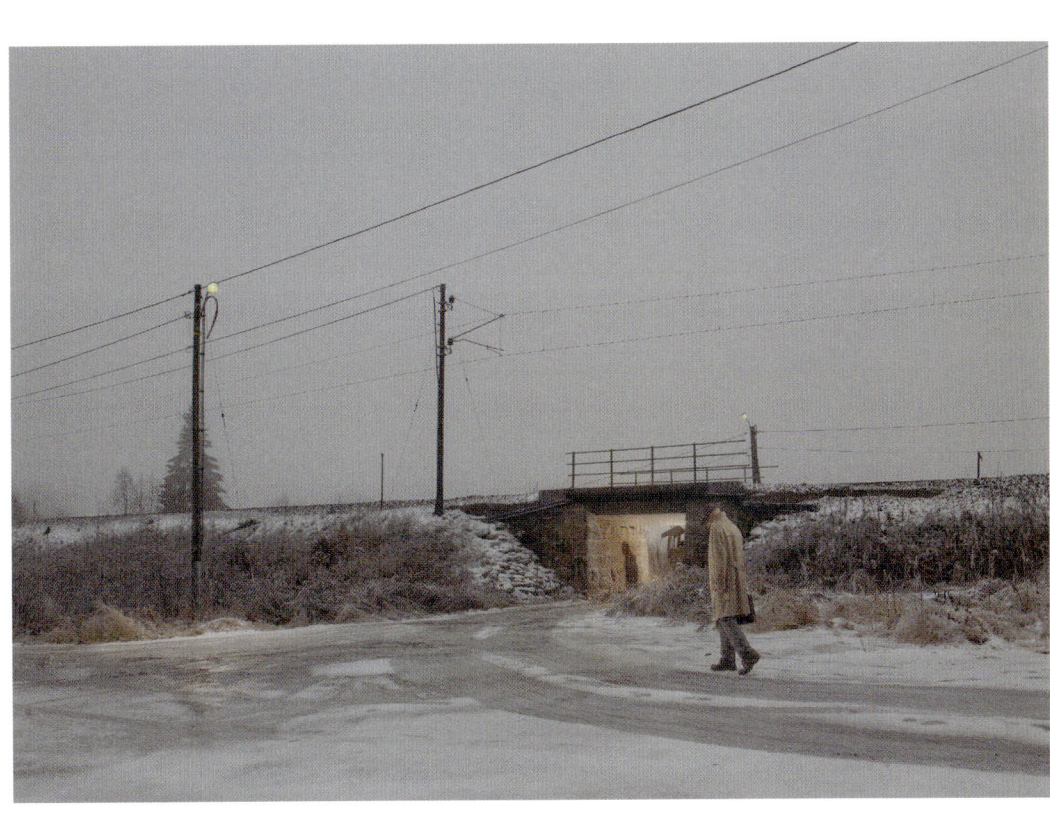

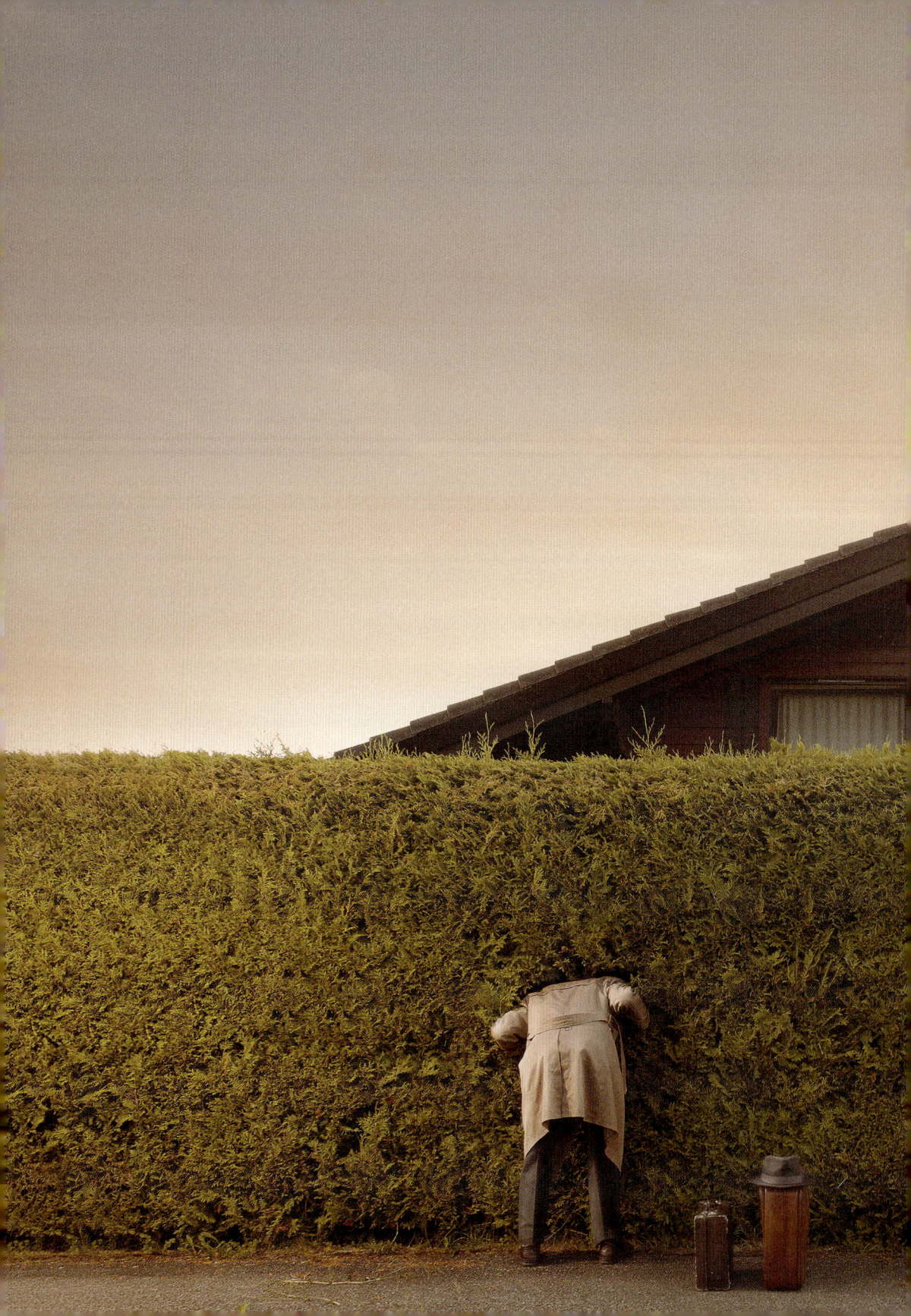

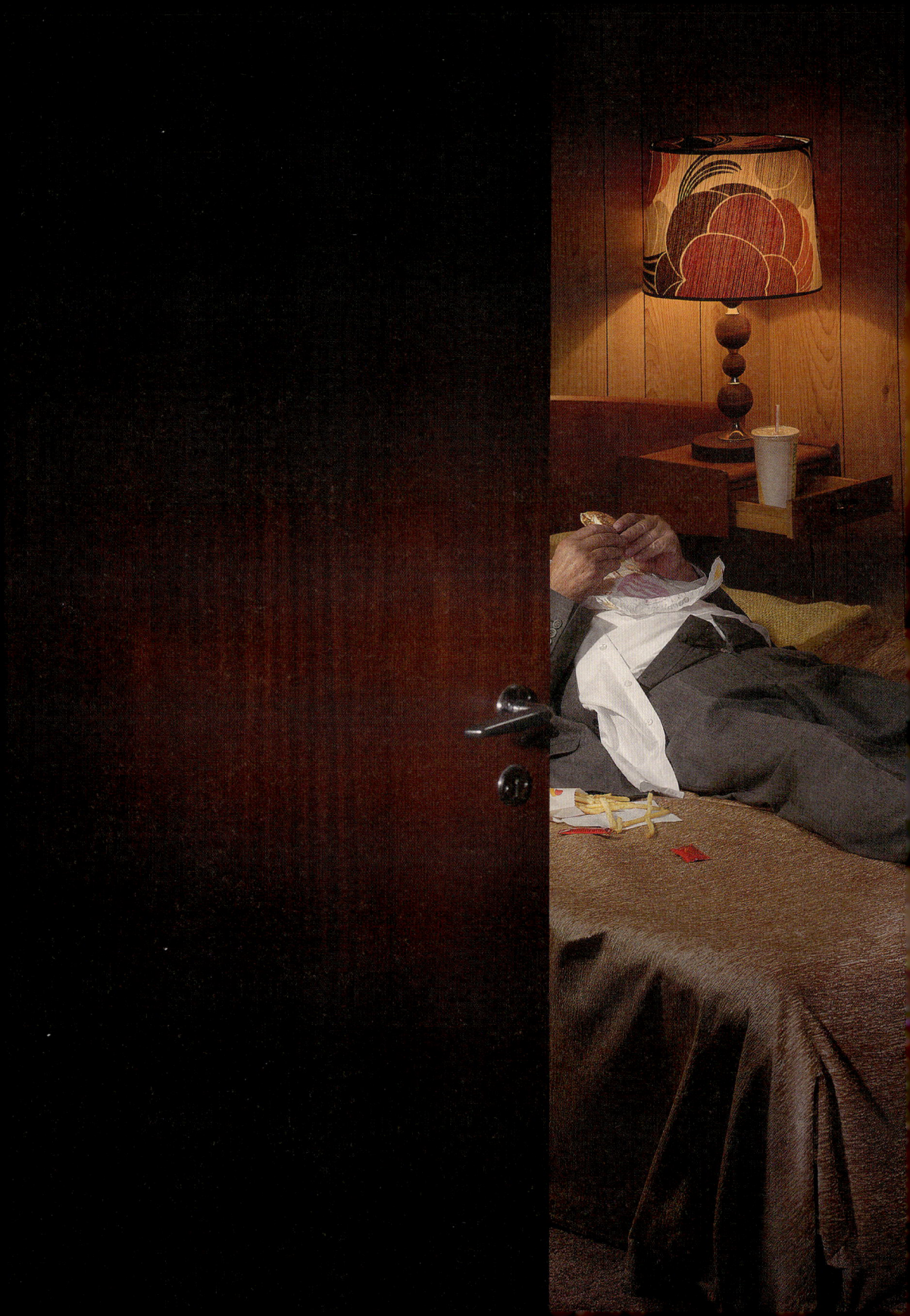

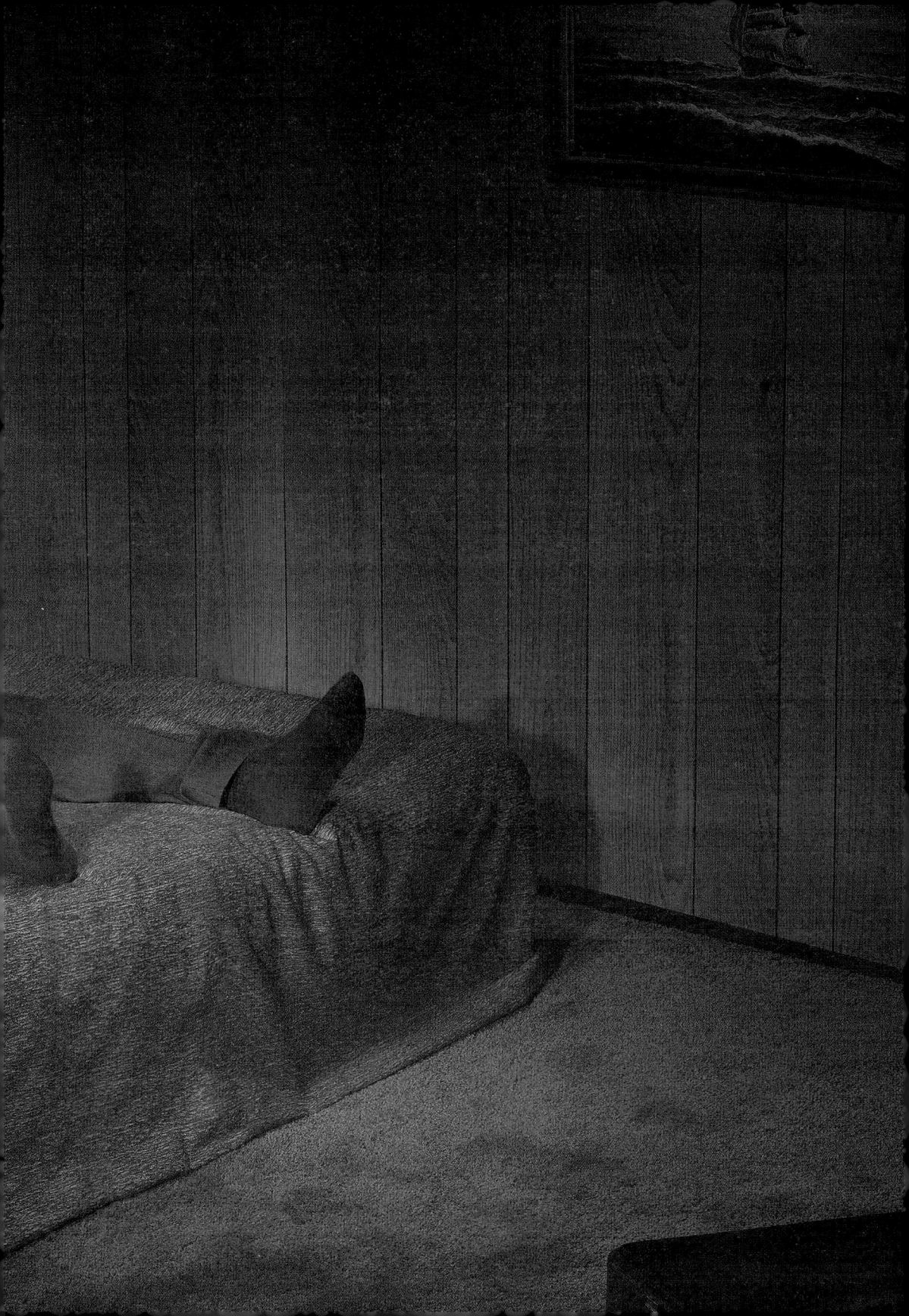

A LONG FORGOTTEN NOCTURNE

2018–2019

In mid 19th Century Europe, artists from the Romantic movement began to focus on the beauty and majesty of nature and everyday scenes of rural life.

"A long forgotten nocturne" is not only an ode to the romantic period but a continuance of the artistic movement shot with a unique, contemporary eye.

With the use of theatrical light and vivid color juxtapositions, Ole Marius' work emphasizes the mystery and duality of rural life in the modern world.

Like the painters of old, Ole Marius travelled through out his rural Norway capturing isolated, disregarded locations wishing to highlight the unique, latent beauty of these places before they vanish.

Old farms and other buildings, which are now forgotten in the modern age, are resurrected using light and the magic of nature, to create an idyllic and mysterious tableau.

Much like the Romantic movement, this series is a reaction to a revolution, in this case the digital revolution that has marked a complete shift in our society.

A society that places little value on the simplicity and beauty of rural life, but instead focuses on the immediate and ephemeral found in contemporary society.

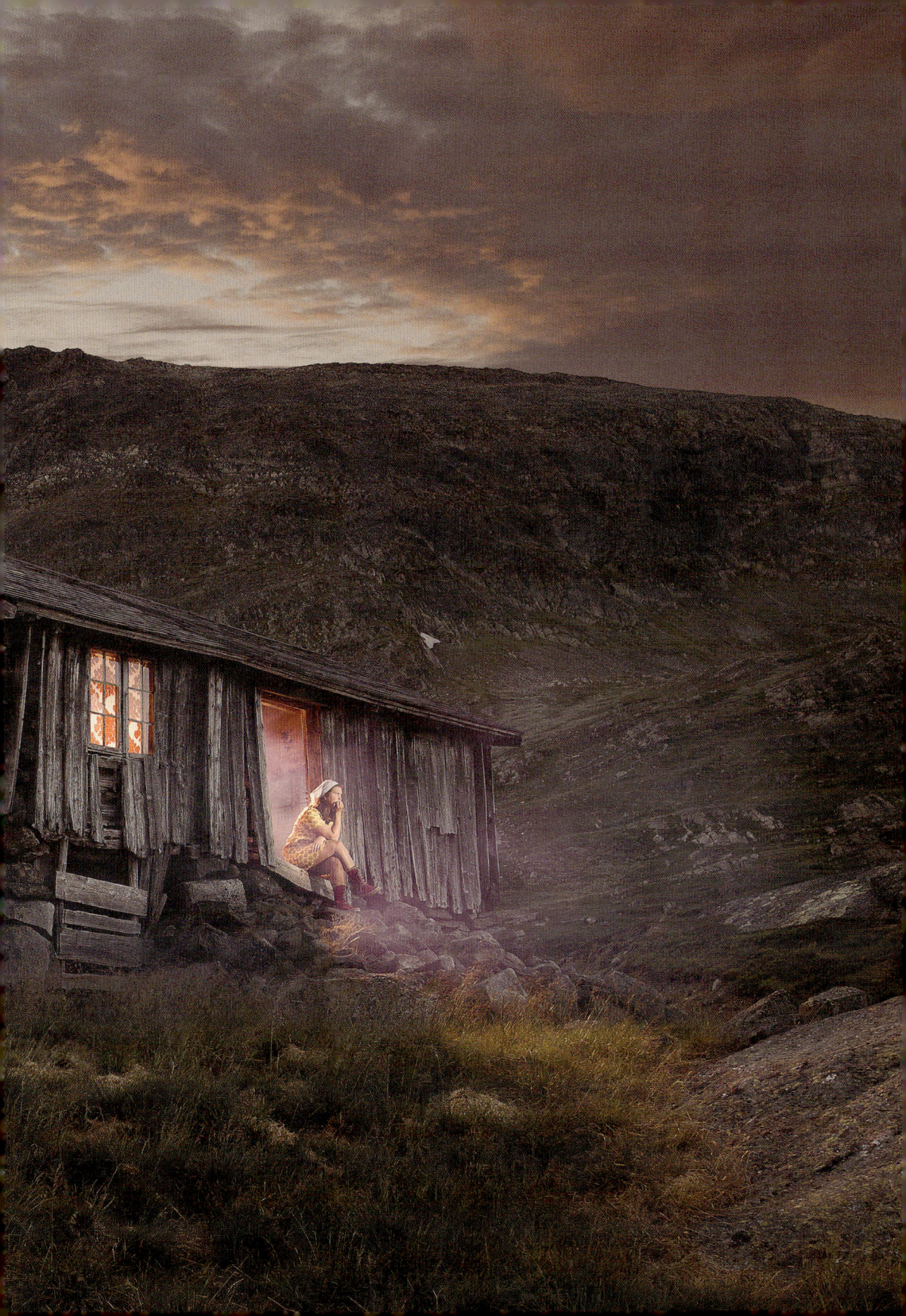

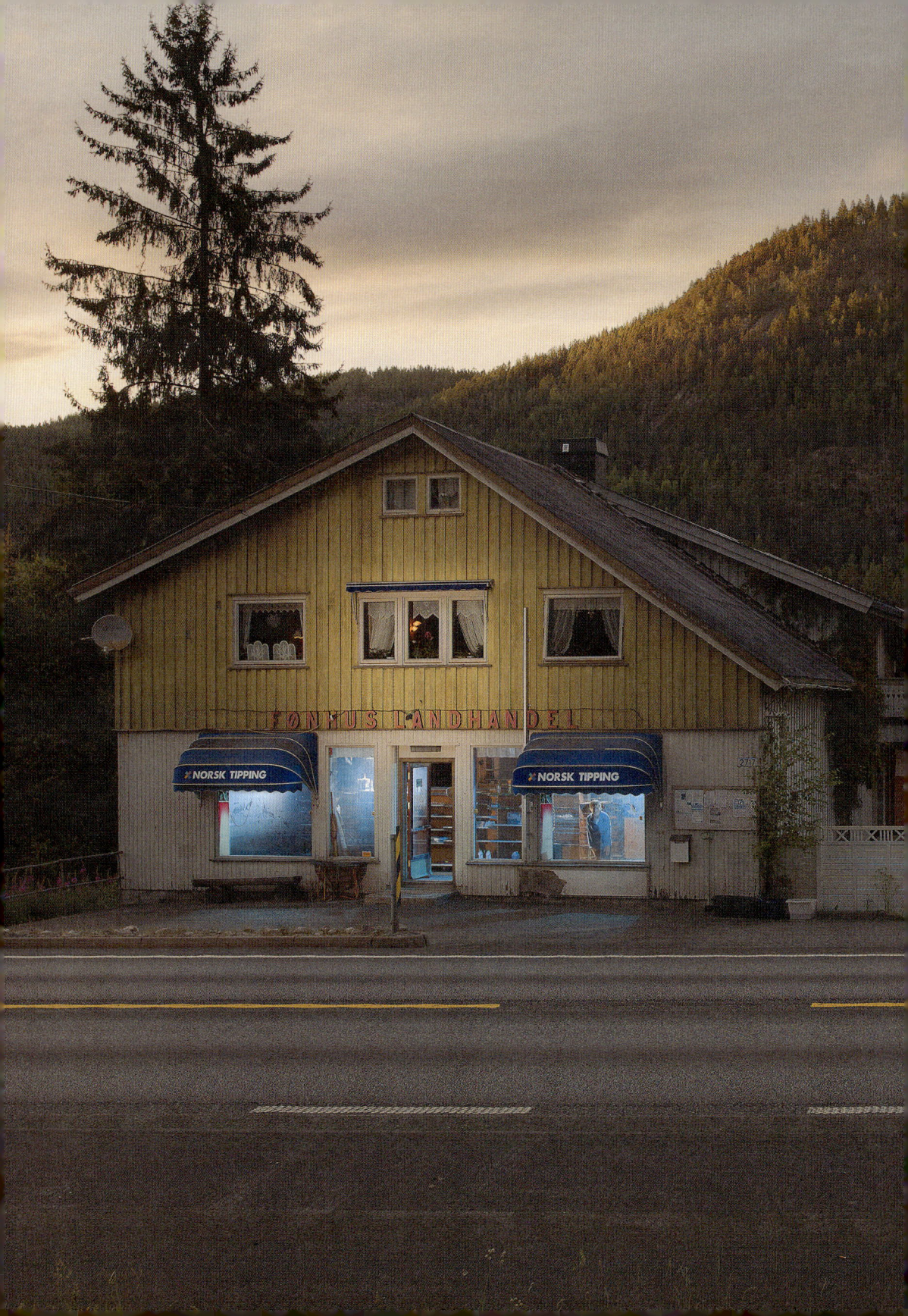

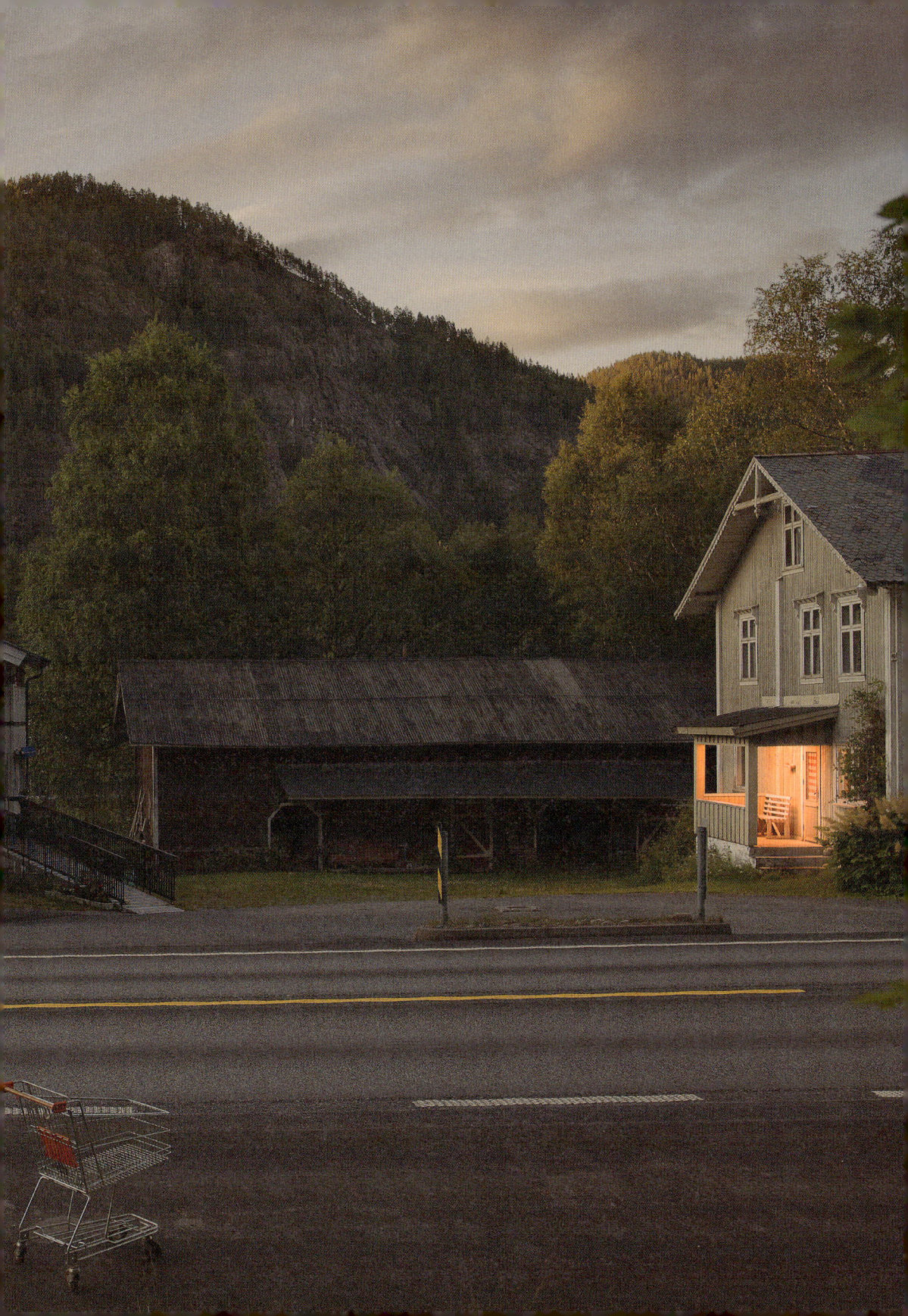

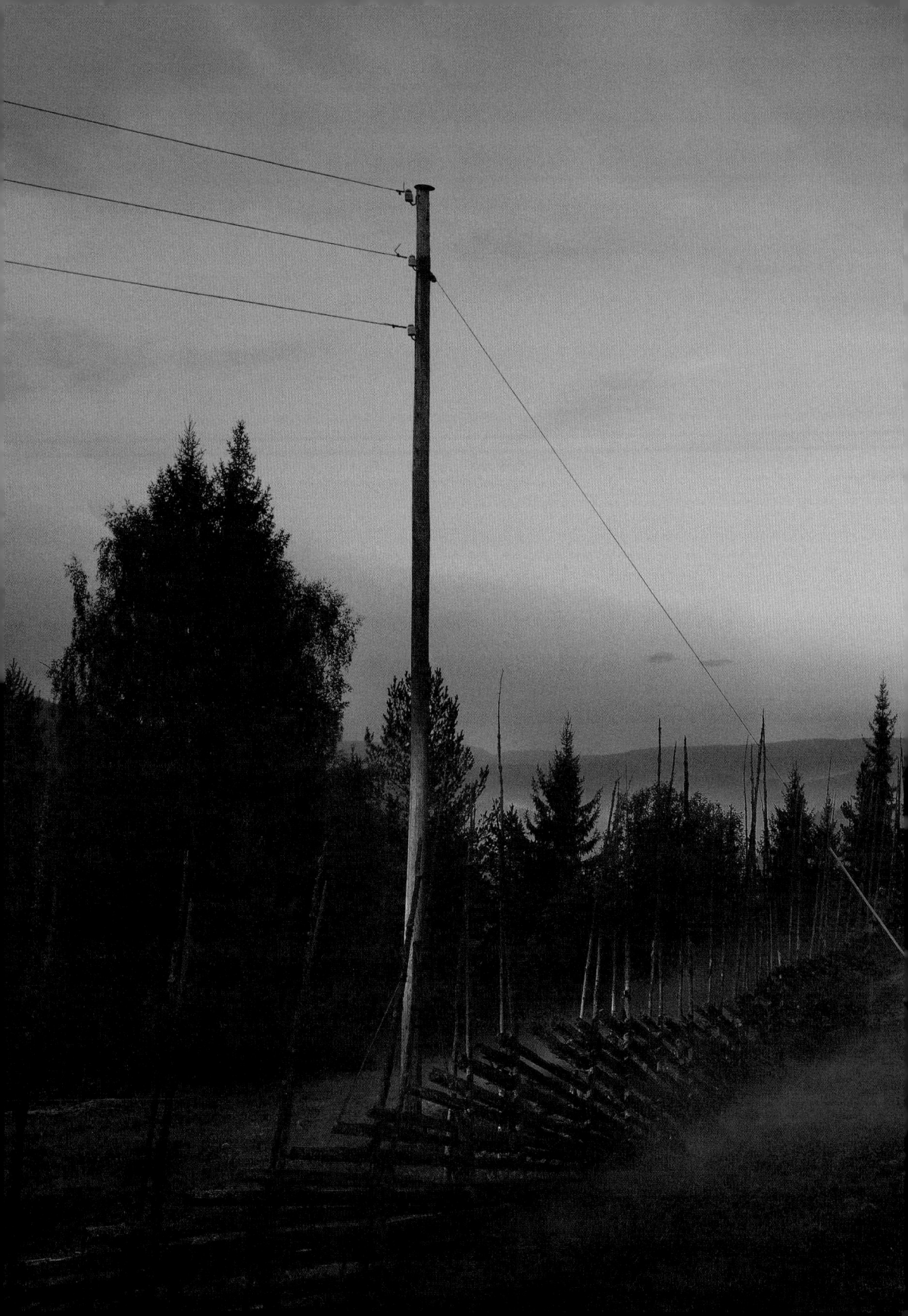

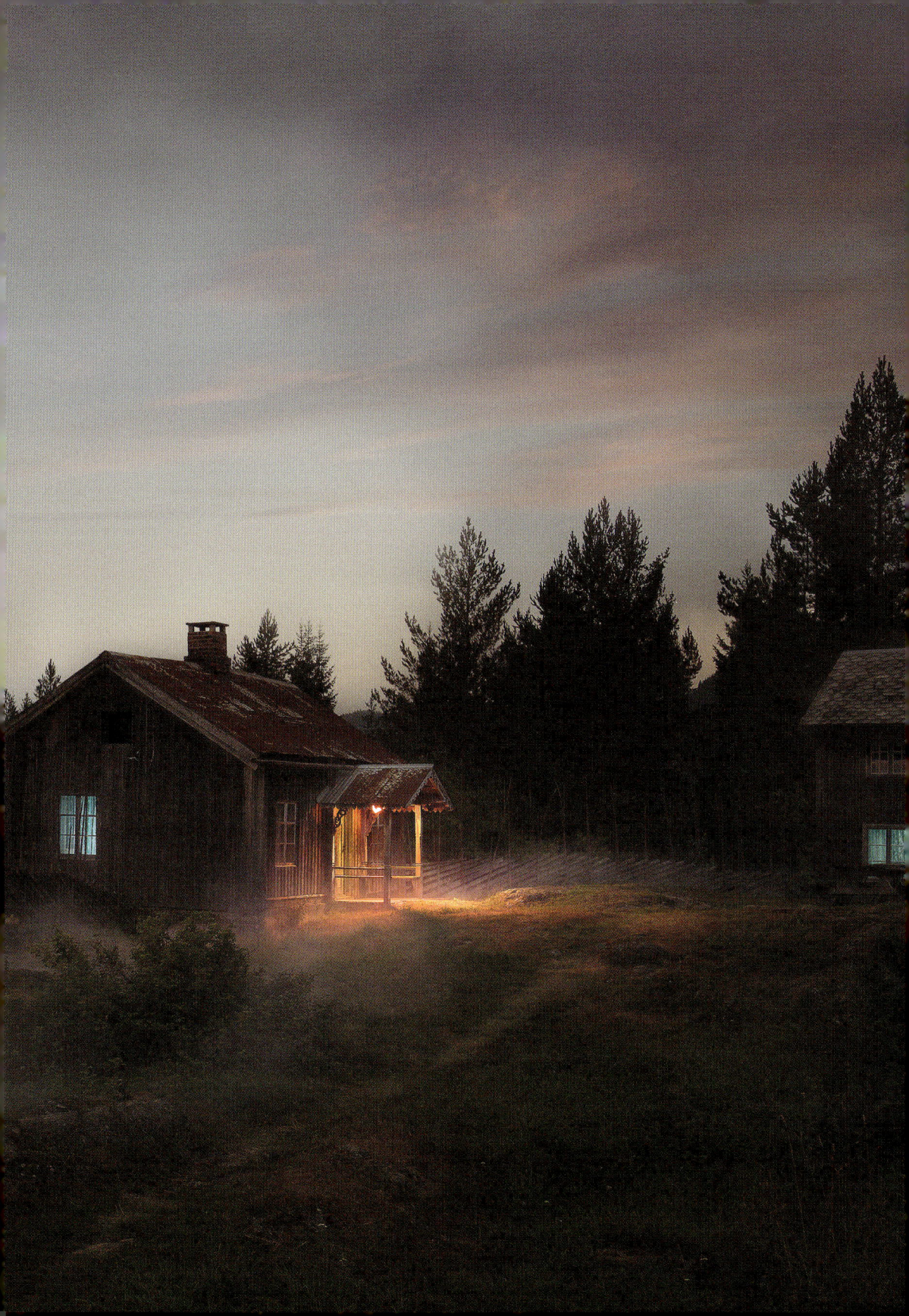

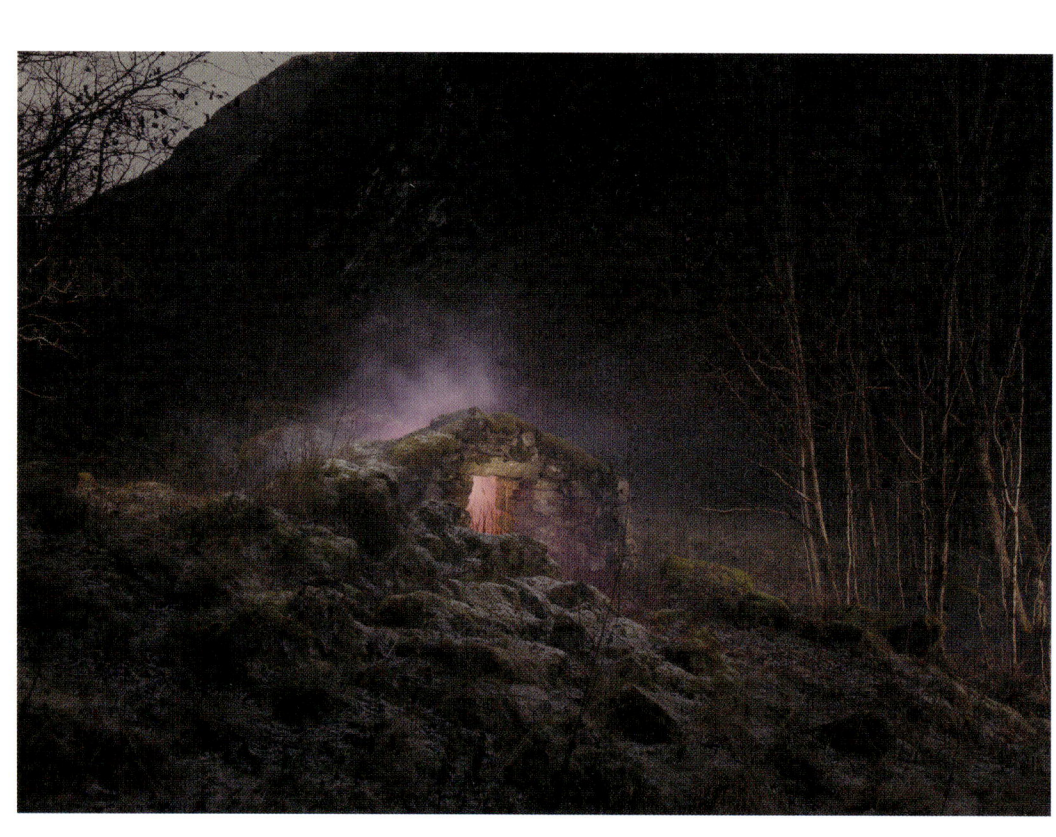

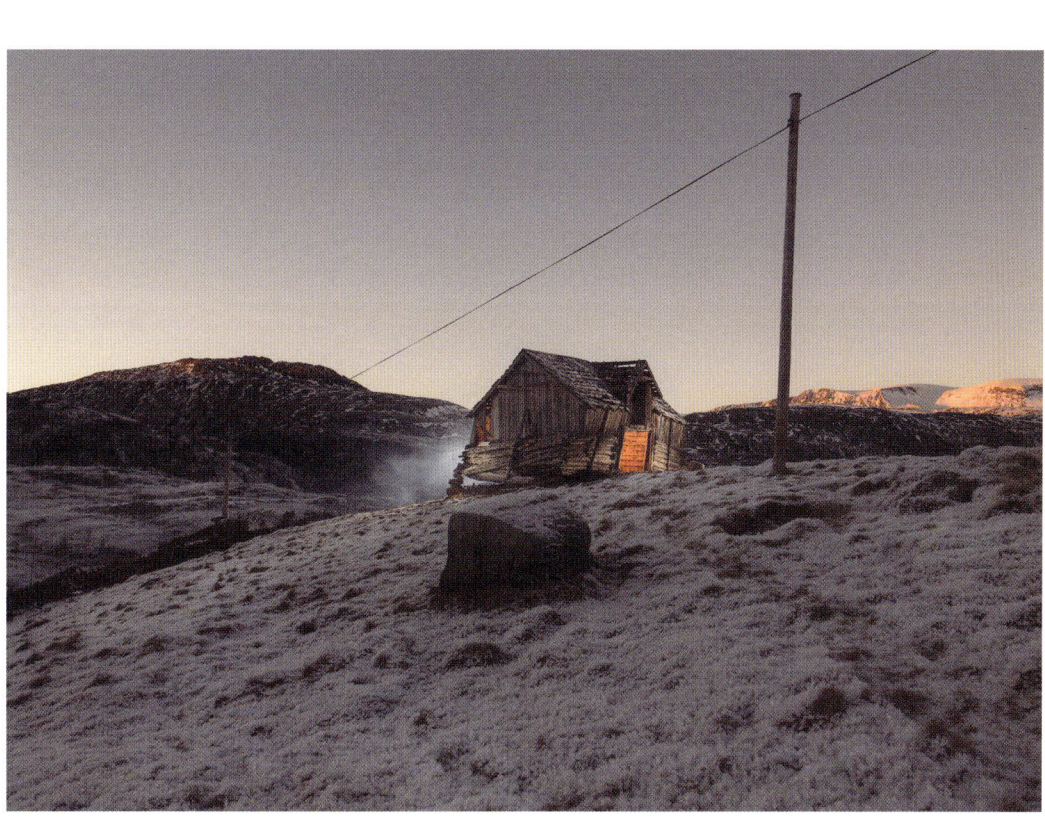

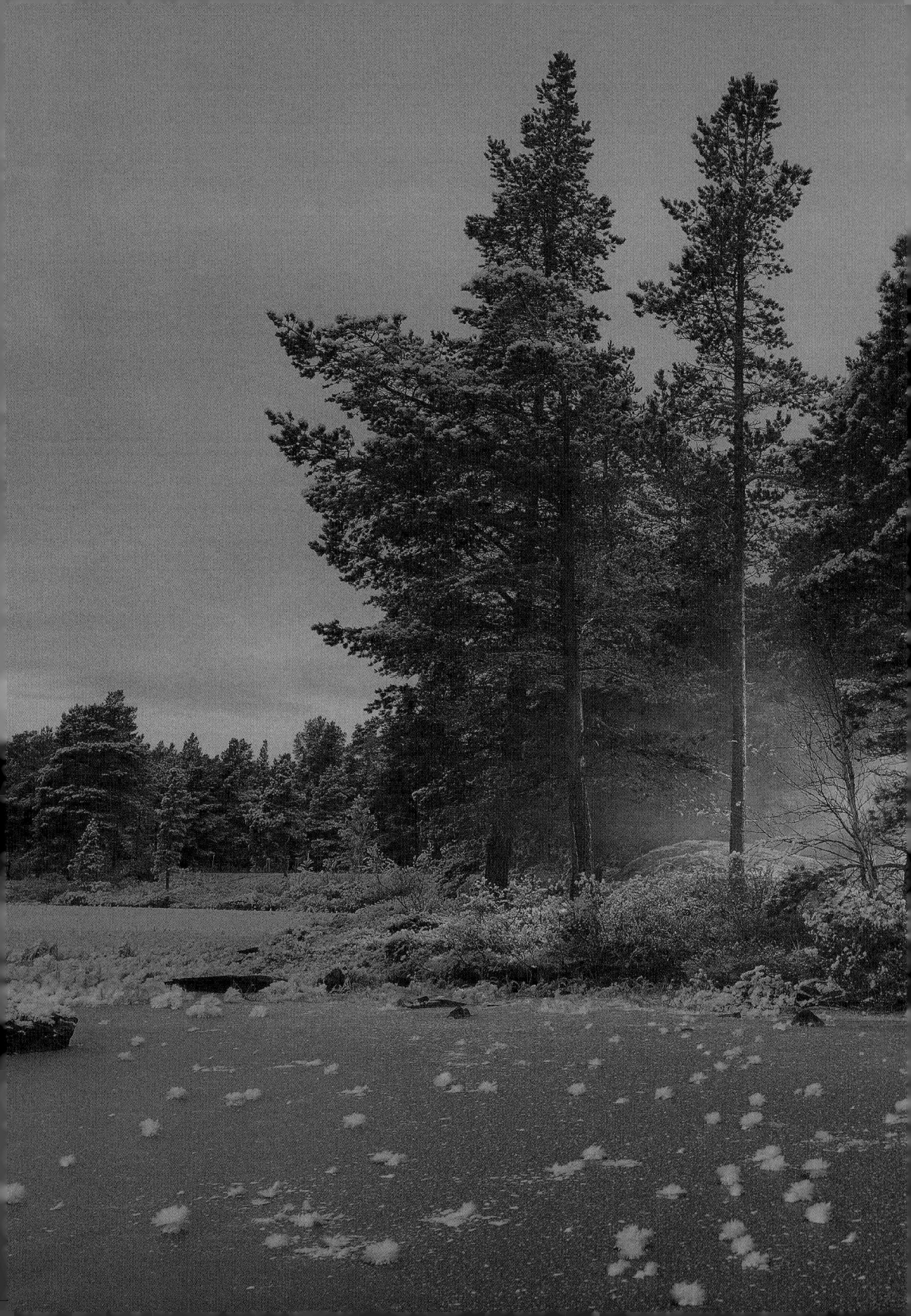

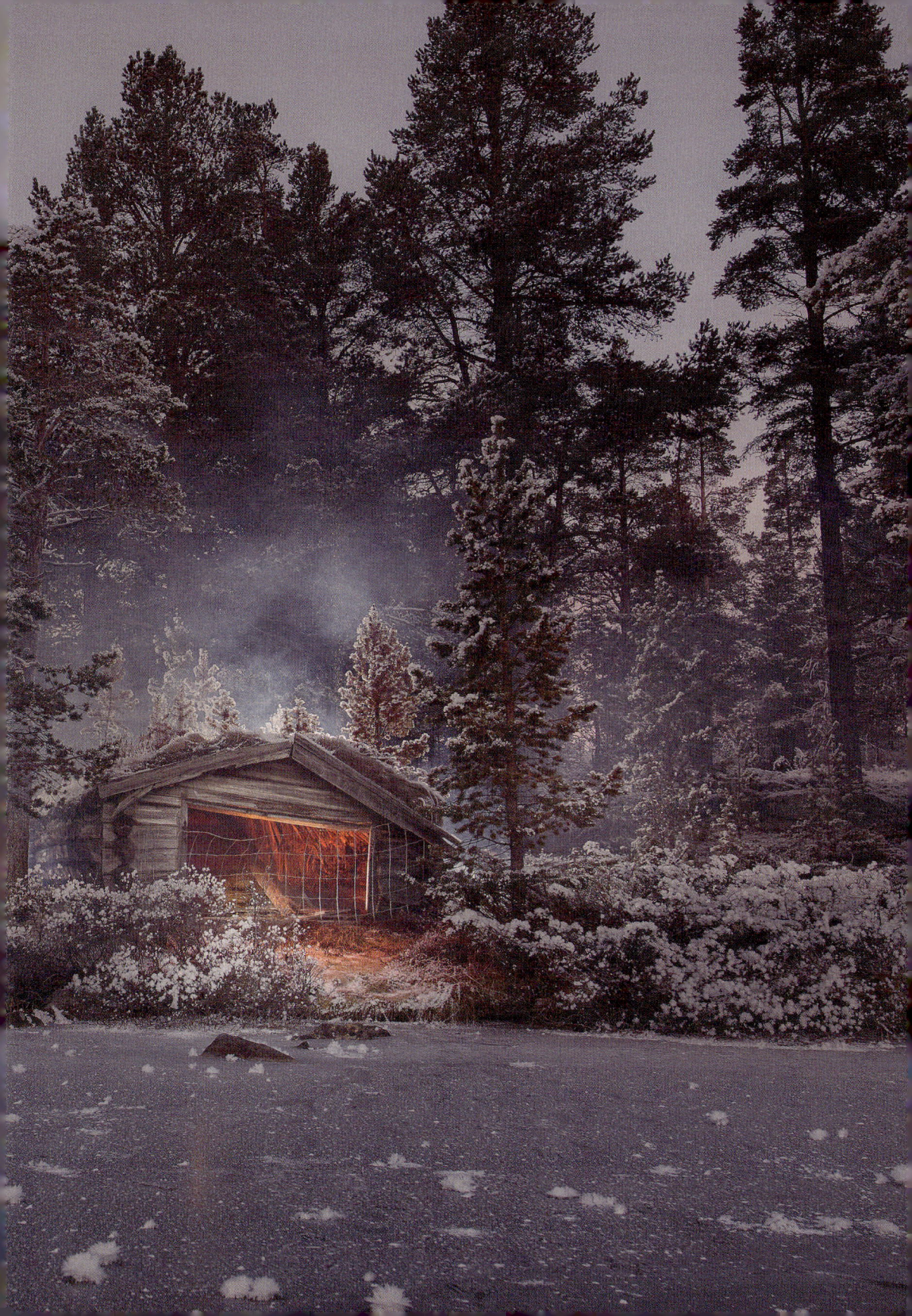

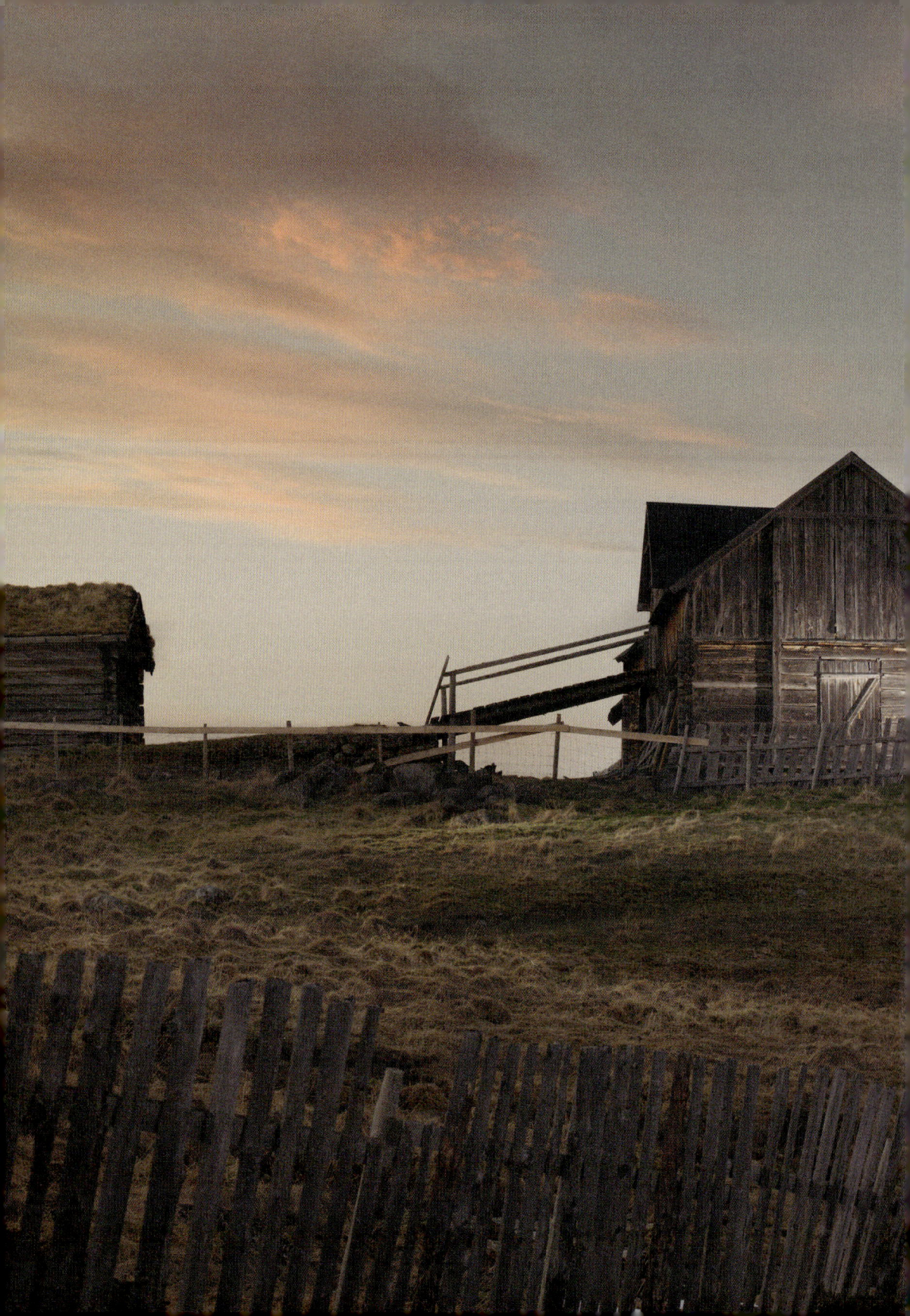

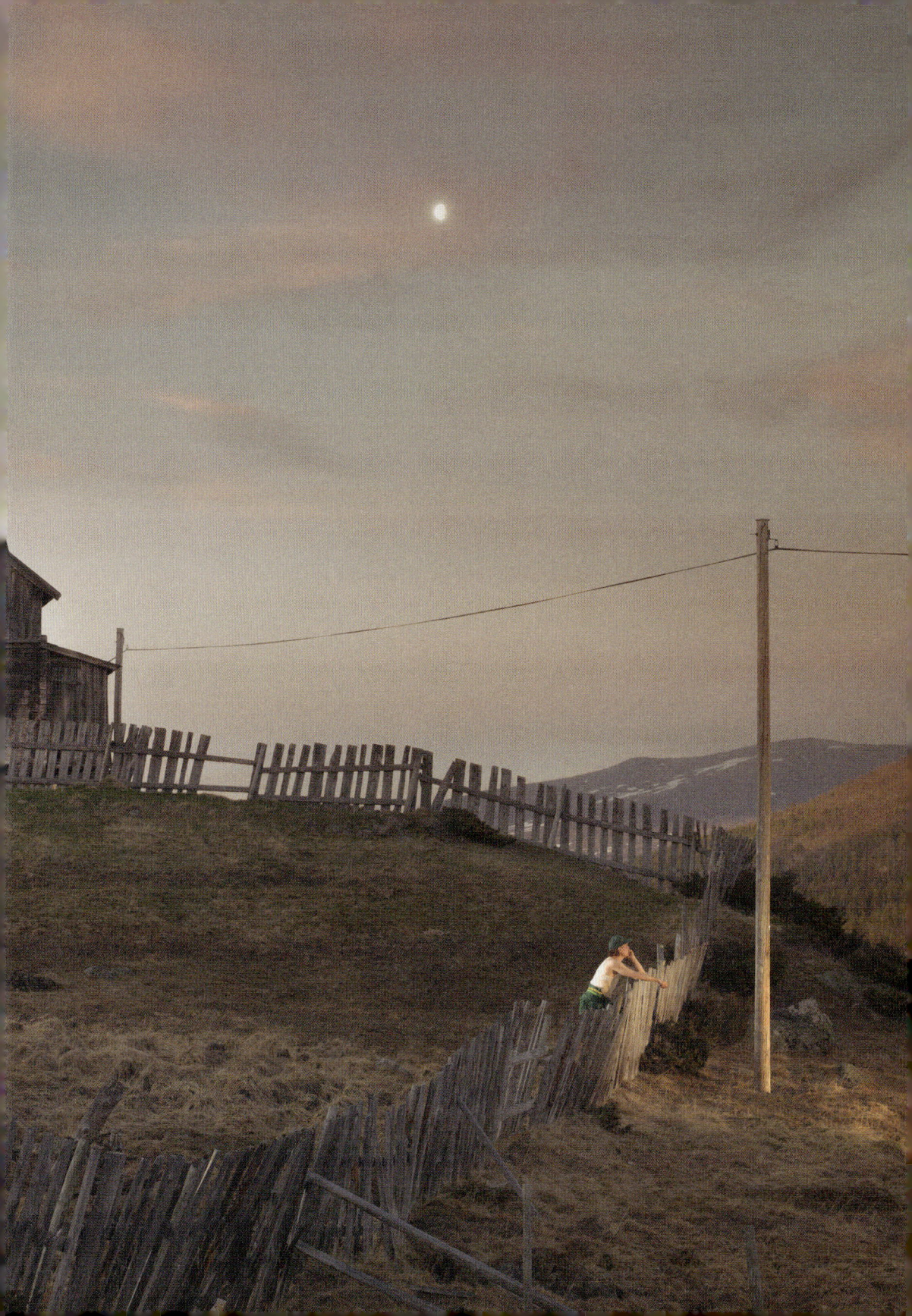

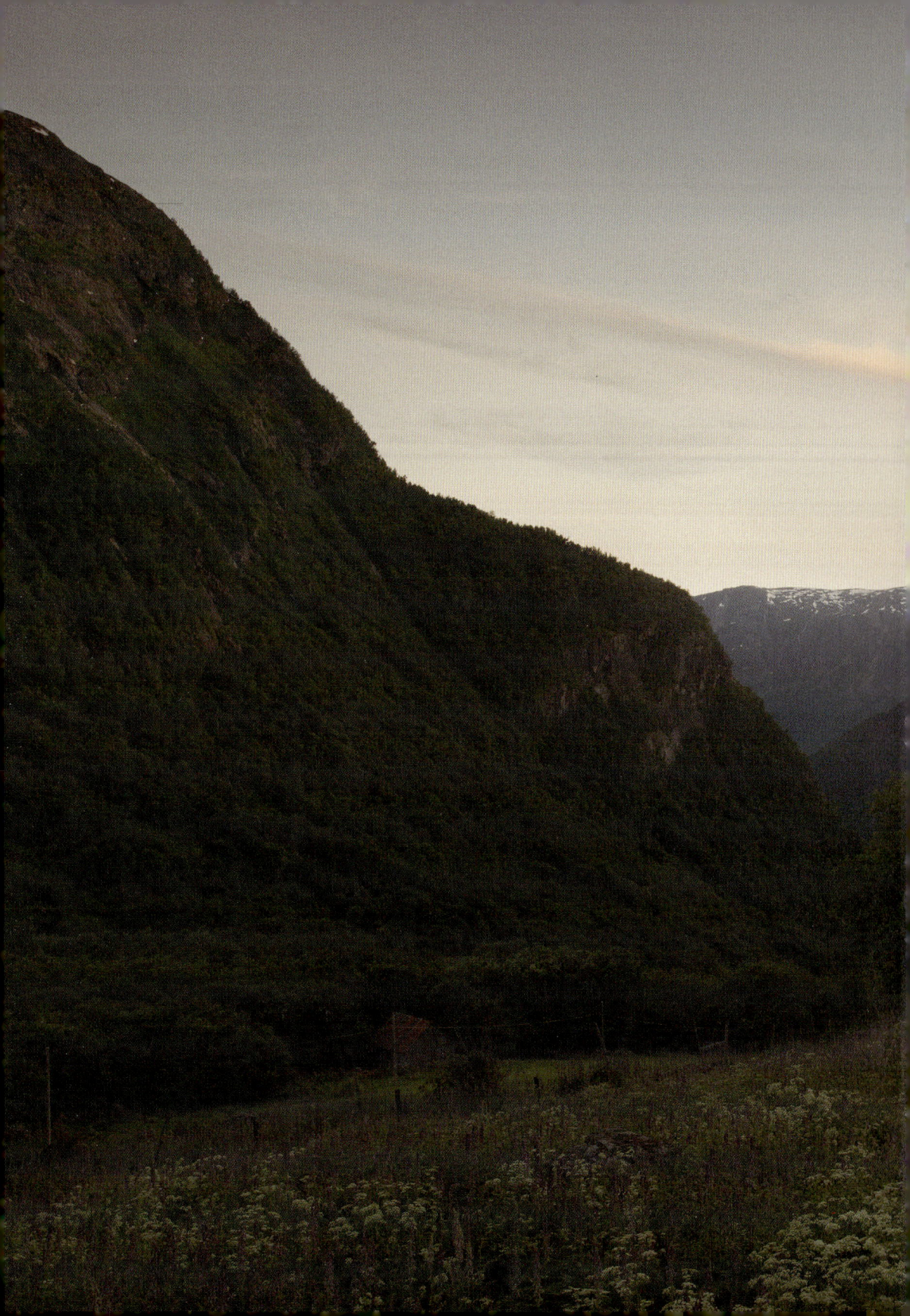

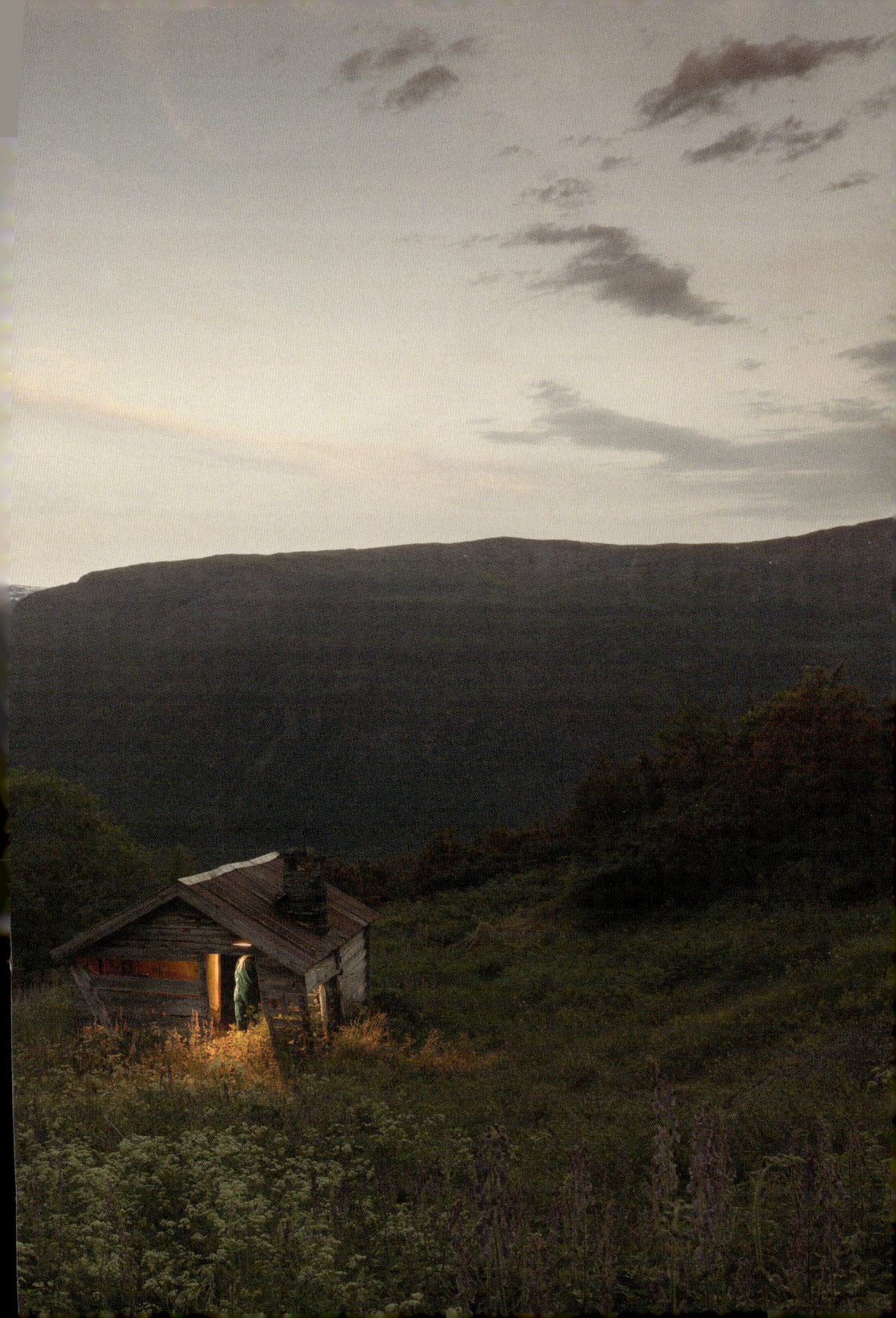

No. Superhero

Published by New Heroes & Pioneers
Photography: Ole Marius Joergensen
Creative Direction: Francois Le Bled
Book Design: Daniel Zachrisson
Copy Editing: Matt Porter
Chapter Intro Texts: Vincent Milner

Print and bound by Livonia Print (Latvia)
Legal Deposit December 2020
ISBN 978-91-87815-46-1

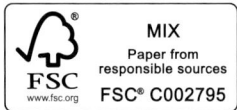

"This book would not be possible without the help and love
of friends and family.

Siena E G Jørgensen, Une H Gjertsen, Bjørn Gjertsen, Kjartan Gjertsen,
Jardar Gjertsen, Folke Hauge, Joakim Sturlasson, Gabrielle Sturlasson,
Espen Sturlasson, Kristian Valen-Sendstad, Guttorm Wiik, Stein K Bjoergo,
Håkon Walnum, Per Christian Thyldum, Ola Hoseth, Øyvind Ovesen,
Ivar Hagerup with family, Scott Baker, Vincent Milner

Thank you."

– Ole Marius Joergensen

COLLECTIVE SHORTS
by NHP PUBLISHING